Contents

List of figures

List of tables

Pathways to permanence for black, Asian and mixed ethnicity children

Julie Selwyn, David Quinton,
Perlita Harris, Dinithi Wijedasa,
Shameem Nawaz and
Marsha Wood

Published by British Association
for Adoption & Fostering
(BAAF)
Saffron House
3rd Floor, 6–10 Kirby Street
London EC1N 8TS
www.baaf.org.uk

Charity registration 275689 (England and Wales)
and SC039337 (Scotland)

© Julie Selwyn, David Quinton, Perlita Harris, Dinithi Wijedasa,
Shameem Nawaz and Marsha Wood, 2010

British Library Cataloguing in Publication Data
A catalogue record for this book is available
from the British Library

ISBN 978 1 905664 87 0

Editorial project management by Shaila Shah, BAAF Publications
Designed by Helen Joubert Associates
Typeset by Avon DataSet Ltd, Bidford on Avon
Printed in Great Britain by TJ International Ltd
Trade distribution by Turnaround Publisher Services,
Unit 3, Olympia Trading Estate, Coburg Road,
London N22 6TZ

BAAF is the leading UK-wide membership
organisation for all those concerned with
adoption, fostering and child care issues.

Acknowledgements

This research would not have been possible without the considerable help of a number of people. We would like to thank the Department for Children, Schools and Families (DCSF) for funding the study and our advisory group for helpful suggestions and comments: Caroline Thomas (Co-ordinator of the Adoption Research Initiative, University of Stirling); Cherilyn Dance (University of Bedfordshire); Elaine Dibben (DCSF Adoption Team); Monica Duck (Post-Adoption Centre, London); Esther Dermott (Sociology Department, University of Bristol); Kate O'Brien (Adoption Planning Manger, Bristol City Council); and Beverley Prevatt-Goldstein (independent consultant).

We are especially grateful to the staff in three local authorities who ensured that children's files were accessible and gave their commitment to the study. Thanks are also due to the social workers who gave up time to be interviewed and who helped us track the progress of children's plans.

Any errors or deficiencies in this study are the sole responsibility of the research team and should not be attributed to any of the advisers. The views expressed in this publication are those of the authors and are not necessarily those of the DCSF.

The Adoption Research Initiative

This series brings together the research studies in the Adoption Research Initiative (ARI), a programme of research on adoption funded by the Department for Children, Schools and Families (DCSF). It is designed to evaluate the impact of the Government's adoption project, including the Adoption and Children Act 2002 and various related policy initiatives. The research initiative is examining how these objectives are being translated into local policies, procedures and practice.

There are seven studies within the Adoption Research Initiative. They address four broad themes: permanency planning and professional decision-making; linking and matching; adoption support; and the costs of adoption. They also complement other recently-reported and current research on the full range of placements for looked after children, including kinship care, foster care, residential care, private fostering and return home.

More information on the Adoption Research Initiative is available on www.adoptionresearchinitiative.org.uk.

Published by BAAF:

- *Enhancing Adoptive Parenting: A test of effectiveness*, Alan Rushton and Elizabeth Monck, 2009
- *Linking and Matching: A survey of adoption agency practice in England and Wales*, Cherilyn Dance, Danielle Ouwejan, Jennifer Beecham and Elaine Farmer, 2010

Executive summary

Background

There is a striking lack of data on minority ethnic* children, how and when they come into care, how decisions are made about their placements and their futures, and what happens to them during their time in care. This study explores the care pathways of such children and considers possible differences in decision-making and outcomes for minority ethnic children in comparison with white children.

Methods

The children in this study came from three local authorities – in London, the Midlands and the North of England – each of which had large minority ethnic populations. The following three sampling frames were utilised:

1. A comparison sample of looked after white and minority ethnic children
This sample was intended to answer questions about differences between white and minority ethnic children in their characteristics, entry to care, service use, decision-making and placement outcomes. A random sample of children under the age of ten who had started to be looked after between 1 April 2002 and 31 March 2003, stratified by ethnicity (48 white and 54 minority ethnic), was obtained. The majority of these children (77%) were less than one year old when referred to Children's Services. Case files were read and data collected.

2. A sample of minority ethnic children with an adoption recommendation
The researchers wanted to see what differences there might be between black, Asian and mixed ethnicity children in their characteristics and how

---

* There is no satisfactory way of referring to minority ethnic children as a group. For ease of reading, black, Asian and mixed ethnicity children has been abbreviated to minority ethnic throughout this summary.

decisions about them were taken forward once the panel had recommended adoption. A second sample was drawn across the three authorities of all the minority ethnic children who had a recommendation for adoption (n = 120) made between 1 April 2005 and 31 March 2006, and data collected on them from case files in exactly the same way as in the comparison study.

3. *Interview sample of social workers*
The research team wanted to track what happened to minority ethnic children once a decision to place them for adoption had been made, and how social workers took ethnicity into account when making difficult placement and matching decisions. To do this, a prospective real-time sample of 50 children, whose case was to be referred to the adoption panel between November 2005 and December 2006, was collected. Their social workers were interviewed before presenting their information to the panel, then at monthly intervals, to track the child's progress towards an adoptive placement. A final telephone call was made in July/August 2007 to find out where the child was placed and if there had been any changes of plan.

Key findings

- The research did not find a *systematic* bias against, or mishandling of, minority ethnic children compared with white children from the time they came to the attention of Children's Services. Nor did the study find a tendency to take minority ethnic children into care more precipitately.
- The majority of the looked after minority ethnic children in the samples were of mixed ethnicity: 57 per cent in the comparison sample, 69 per cent in the adoption recommended sample and 74 per cent in the interview study. These children came from a wide variety of ethnic heritages and it is unhelpful to refer to mixed ethnicity children as if they comprise a meaningful group or community.
- Most of the mixed ethnicity children had white mothers and were thus the outcome of relationships between white women and men from different ethnic backgrounds. In comparison with the other mothers,

the white or mixed ethnicity mothers had experienced the most adversity.

- Mixed ethnicity children's pathways through care were similar to those of white children.
- The small sub-sample of black children came to the notice of Children's Services when they were older compared with the sample of white, Asian or mixed ethnicity children. Some had been in private foster care and/or had been living in several different countries before the first referral was made. Consequently, they were older when they first became looked after. This affected their subsequent careers and they were much less likely than the white or mixed ethnicity children to be adopted.
- The most striking difference for Asian children was the role played by *izzat* (family honour) in the birth parents' impetus to relinquish or abandon children.
- The child's age was the most important predictive factor as to whether a child was adopted or not. The older the child at the time of the adoption recommendation, the less likely it was that he or she would be placed for adoption.
- Children's social workers often had little understanding of the adoption process and many were searching for a two-parent family with children who would match the ethnicity of the child. Some children were not adopted because there was little or no promotion and their social worker believed that adopters could not be found.
- The likelihood of adoption for both the black and the Asian children was low, with plans changing away from adoption for the majority (64%) of the Asian children.
- The quality of the information gathered on these children – for example, core assessments and adoption medicals or health plans – was poor (although it was not good for any ethnic group, including white children).
- Professional disagreement over "same-race" placements sometimes arose when white foster carers applied to adopt minority ethnic children for whom they had cared since birth, and/or where attachments had formed between the carers and the child.

- Social workers evidently struggled with how to think about mixed ethnicity children. The common approach (often reported to be agency policy) was to view the children as "Black", even when the ethnicity of the father was not known, or when the child had been brought up entirely within a white culture.
- Social workers used the term "ethnicity" interchangeably with "culture". When discussing culture, they were often referring only to ethnic categorisations, even though crude ethnic labels did not necessarily contribute to understanding a child's culture.

1   Background and literature review

There are a number of beliefs about black, Asian and mixed ethnicity children in the care system, their placements, permanence options and outcomes. It is widely thought that they are over-represented amongst looked after children; are subject to more delays in the process of achieving permanence; that their psychosocial outcomes depend crucially on careful matching between the physical and cultural heritage of their birth parents and of those who foster or adopt them; and that they are less likely to be placed for adoption and more likely to be in kinship care or long-term foster care.

Some of these claims are better evidenced than others. Indeed, much of this debate is conducted in the absence of any systematic data. The research reported in this book is intended to begin to address these gaps.

"Race", ethnicity and culture

Debates about definitions, terms and underlying beliefs about "race" and ethnicity have been fierce, and the topic remains a contested and contentious area of study. Since legislation requires local authorities to consider a child's racial origin and cultural background when placing for adoption, it might be thought that these concepts are well defined and that a clearly understood set of meanings is attached to them by those who drafted and approved the legislation. This may be the case but we have not been able to find definitions in the practice guidelines.

Both professional and everyday discourses, as well as legislative and official bodies, use the term "race" freely. Thus we talk about "transracial placements", "racial identity", matching on "race", and we have race relations legislation. The term "race" is thus embedded in official and everyday thinking. This topic is discussed in more detail in our companion report on matching (Quinton, 2010), but a brief discussion of "race" is in order here.

The idea of sorting humans into distinct "races" arose in the 18th and

19th centuries in the encounter between European colonial domination and the development of scientific classifications of the natural world. It involved the hierarchical ordering of plants and animals into groups based on *differences*, as in the idea of species and sub-species. In the 20th century, classifications of peoples based on physical type became attached to geographical areas, so that the idea of "race" came to involve a physical distinctness – most commonly skin tone – associated with an area of geographical origin. It thus united two features of "otherness": that a group is physically distinguishable and that it comes from somewhere else (Marks, 2008). This meaning is still apparent in current usage and belief.

Recently the idea that this otherness is something immutable or "essential" has been linked to a misreading of the genetics of inheritance even though, as Lewontin pointed out as long ago as 1972, it is not possible to specify a set of defining genes for race. Moreover, the amount of genetic variation within supposedly similar populations ("races") is greater than that between different ones (see also Dupré, 2008).

The predominant consensus amongst geneticists and sociologists is that the term "race" is a social construction that is not biologically meaningful. Rather, as Haslanger (2008, p 65) has observed, its use reflects relationships of power, domination and oppression, through which a group can be treated differentially in economic and social ways because of '. . . observed or imagined bodily features presumed to be evidence of an ancestral link to a certain geographic region'. The continued use of the term in social policy and political discussions seems to be only appropriate when it refers to abuses of power and to actions deriving from mistaken beliefs about essential differences. That is, when it refers to "racisms".

Although "race" is still used in discussions on child placement, there has been a general move to replace it with the term "ethnicity", because this potentially avoids the trap of essentialist arguments and takes language, religion and social and family patterns into account. For this reason, we have used "ethnicity" throughout this report. However, we have become aware that this term can itself easily become an acceptable proxy for "race", as can other alternatives such as "ancestry" or "heritage", and thus retain essentialist elements. Even when "ethnicity" is used without these undertones, it can still be accompanied by mistaken ideas that an ethnic culture is both homogeneous and unchanging.

Despite these concerns, we needed to have some way of referring to the children who are the focus of this study, even though we are aware of the limitations of all descriptive labels, especially in aggregate. As Modood and his colleagues have pointed out, there are no satisfactory terms for referring to black, Asian and mixed ethnicity children as a group, because they are so diverse in physical and cultural heritage (Modood *et al*, 1997). However, for ease of reading we have chosen to use the term "minority ethnic" in the chapters that follow, rather than "black and minority ethnic" (BME). This acronym is one that many people dislike because of its diminution of the categories to which it refers and because it double-refers to the black group. We also recognise that some children are not a "minority" in their own local authority areas and that the word "ethnic" has begun to have more negative connotations, as for example in the term "ethnic cleansing".

Throughout this book, lower case is used when referring to "black" and "white" as ethnic categories, but these terms are capitalised in the text (e.g. "Black") in the context of political claims. Also, we have used the term "African-Caribbean" throughout this study, except when we are referring to, or quoting from, other studies; in these cases, we have used the terminology employed by the authors of those studies, for example, Jamaican, Caribbean, Black Caribbean. The definitions we have chosen to use for ethnicity and culture are to be found in Appendix I, as are the ethnic categories used in the 2001 Census and these have informed the way we have approached the data and analysis.

Background

In England, there is a striking lack of data on minority ethnic children in the care system, how and when they come into care, how decisions are made about their placements and their futures, and what happens to them in their care pathways. One reason for this lack of evidence is the absence, until very recently, of the recording of ethnicity in official statistics and Children's Services case records. Local authorities have only been required to collect data on the ethnicity of children receiving services since 2000/1 and are still not required to collect data on religion or language.

Unlike the USA, there are national data on children's ethnicity only at certain points of a child's care pathway. It was only in 2009 that data on ethnicity were collected nationally at the point of referral. This means that accurate estimates of over- or under-representation of minority ethnic children in the care system and studies of "care pathways" have been hard to come by. Several studies (Barn *et al*, 1997; Dutt and Philipps, 2000; Lowe *et al*, 2002) have highlighted large gaps in the recording, by social workers, of a child's ethnicity, religion and culture and the impact this has on planning at every level.

Another reason is that practice and research cannot keep up with fast-changing demographics. There has been a growth in the number of mixed-ethnic adult partnerships and marriages. Over half of African-Caribbean men and 20 per cent of black African men are in a relationship with a white woman (Platt, 2009). These changes mean that those who define themselves as singularly Caribbean are likely to decline over time, as increasingly complex ethnicities emerge among those with some element of Caribbean heritage.

Consequently, there has also been a rise in the number of mixed ethnicity children being born. Census 2001 found that almost four per cent of all under-five-year-olds in England and Wales were of mixed ethnicity and that one quarter of *all* the under-five-years-old minority ethnic population were of mixed ethnicity. This is a huge demographic shift in the population. What is most striking is not just the growth of the mixed ethnicity child population as a percentage of the total population – but also as a percentage of the minority ethnic population. The growth in people who consider themselves to be of mixed ethnicity raises questions about how identity is conceptualised and challenges boundaries based on identification by professionals as either Black or White (Wood, 2009).

Thirdly, with a few notable exceptions (Barn *et al*, 1997; Thoburn *et al*, 2000), there is a lack of studies focusing on minority ethnic children. For this reason, evidence has come from piecing together data from the low numbers of minority ethnic children in studies sampling from more broadly defined populations of looked after children. Not only are these data-aggregating exercises problematic because of differences in methods, definitions and measures, they also make it almost inevitable that minority ethnic children are treated as a single group rather than allowing for differences between different heritages. Aggregation may be masking important differences, experiences and trajectories.

Many studies in England have found that there are more looked after minority ethnic children than would be expected, given their proportions in the national population (e.g. Bebbington and Miles, 1989; Thoburn *et al*, 2005). However, it is also known that living in poverty is associated with contact with the child welfare system, so minority ethnic children, who are more likely to live in poorer areas, might be expected to be over-represented.

A recent analysis of national datasets (Owen and Statham, 2009) found a more complex picture. Ethnicity made a big difference beyond the differences stemming from where a child happened to live. It was evident that children from some ethnic groups did start to be looked after at rates different from what might be expected given their numbers in the population. In particular, black and mixed ethnicity children were over-represented while there were far fewer Asian children looked after than would be expected. Different ethnic groups first entered care at different ages, they remained looked after for different lengths of time, and they varied with regards to the likelihood of their being adopted or returned to their parents. Mixed ethnicity children were the youngest (five years on average) at entry to care and the oldest were black African children (nine years on average). In the year ending 31 March 2009, 76 per cent of looked after children were white, eight per cent mixed ethnicity, seven per cent black, five per cent Asian and three per cent from other ethnic groups (DCSF, 2009). Owen and Statham (2009) comment on the complexity of the patterns and note that large national datasets are not able to provide the reasons for the observed disproportionalities.

One of the reasons why some minority ethnic children enter care later might be related to differential social work practice. Anecdotal accounts, as well as evidence from investigations such as the Climbié Inquiry, suggest that professionals involved with minority ethnic families because of child protection concerns may be more reluctant to act because of fears of offending community sensibilities or fears of being accused of racism

(Scorer, 2005; Bernard and Gupta, 2006). An analysis of child deaths and serious injury through abuse and neglect (Brandon *et al*, 2008) found that lack of cultural knowledge and misplaced sensitivity could 'dampen down the kind of professional curiosity essential if interacting risk factors were to be considered' (p101). However, other research studies have found little evidence of a differential response (Brophy *et al*, 2003; Williams and Soydan, 2005).

Research on the reasons why minority ethnic children come into care

Small samples sizes have hampered our understanding of how and why minority ethnic children enter the care system. Questions have been raised about whether minority ethnic children enter care more rapidly than white children, have different patterns of referral from statutory agencies, and are less likely to self-refer than white families (Barn, 1993; Barn and Sinclair, 2001).

Statistics from the Department for Children, Schools and Families (DCSF) for England (2008) show that abuse or neglect were the main reasons for children from all ethnic groups entering care during the year ending 31 March 2008. This was especially the case for Bangladeshi (71%), Pakistani (64%) and about 62 per cent of white British and mixed ethnicity children. This was less frequently the reason for black children (52%) and those of any other ethnic group (43%). Absent parenting (a category often used for asylum-seeking children) was more likely to be the reason why some ethnic groups of children became looked after, particularly those categorised as "Chinese" or "other white", "other Asian" and "other ethnicities" (Owen and Statham, 2009).

There is some evidence that minority ethnic children are more likely to come to the attention of child protection services once in crisis, and not to have been supported beforehand (Barn *et al*, 1997; Hunt *et al*, 1999). There has also been repeated concern in the literature about lack of communication between key agencies and a lack of relevant services for minority ethnic families (Hunt *et al*, 1999; O'Neale, 2000; Becher and Hussain, 2003; Brophy *et al*, 2003).

There is also in the literature a hypothesis that strongly gendered norms placing women in a subordinate position within African families may operate to constrain mothers in their ability to protect their children in the context of domestic violence (Bernard and Gupta, 2006). There is, however, little research evidence to support or contradict this. Masson and colleagues (2008) found a similar rate of concerns about domestic violence across all ethnic groups in a sample of 400 cases of children. Although the study contained a small sample of minority ethnic children (52), concerns about drug misuse were much more likely to be recorded in the case files of black Caribbean mothers and much less likely to be recorded as a concern in the case of black African or South Asian mothers. Crime, neglect/repeat accidents, housing difficulties, and maternal mental health problems were also more frequently recorded for black Caribbean mothers, and nearly a third had a history of being in care themselves compared to 17 per cent of all mothers in the sample. Concerns about physical abuse or over-chastisement were recorded less frequently for black Caribbean mothers but at an above average rate for black African and South Asian mothers. However, no consistent picture emerges from studies (Chand and Thoburn, 2005; Bernard and Gupta, 2006).

Evidence from an NSPCC study (2007) involving 500 British Asian families suggests that one reason for the low numbers of children from this community becoming looked after may be a particular reluctance to report suspected child abuse, due to fears of the negative impact this would have on the child or their own family. Over a third of those interviewed had suspected a child was being abused but nearly half of these did nothing about their concerns.

Korbin's cross-cultural review (2002) suggests that some children are more at risk of maltreatment than others:

- children whose health status is inferior to that of their siblings;
- disabled children;
- excess or unwanted children;
- children born in unusual, stigmatised or difficult circumstances;
- children of the "wrong" gender (females in some cultures, males in others);
- children with difficult behaviour and personality characteristics;
- children in families with poor social supports.

Korbin's review stresses the importance of social networks in making child rearing a shared concern and diminishing the consequences for children with aggressive parents. The lack of social networks, especially grandparents for some minority ethnic groups (Barn *et al*, 2006), may reduce the protective environment and increase the risk of abuse.

Social workers' responses to ethnic differences

How social workers respond to ethnic differences has received little research attention. Williams and Soydan (2005) found in a cross-national study of social workers' responses that they all stated that they would respond in similar ways, irrespective of the family's ethnic background, when considering child protection vignettes. However, social workers tended to favour psychological and behavioural explanations over social structural considerations. Issues connected to poverty, housing conditions, displacement, torture, exclusion or racism were omitted from their explanatory framework. However, what social workers say and what they do may not be similar.

Concern has been expressed that minority ethnic families are too often pathologised with workers over-relying on cultural stereotypes (Ahmed, 1990; Thanki, 1994), and that families receive more speedy punitive responses with less preventative work (Creighton, 1992; Barn, 1993). Stereotypes are also a factor in cultural relativism – a view that all cultures are equally valid and no social worker has the right to pass judgement on cultural practices (Channer and Parton, 1990; Corby, 1993). As Williams and Soydan (2005) note, this leads to a *laissez faire* approach and a lack of adequate response, which has led to some high-profile child deaths.

Research on the permanent placement of minority ethnic children

A recent UK study (Farmer and Moyers, 2008) has noted that minority ethnic children, in particular, are more likely than white children to have long-term foster care as their plan rather than adoption and less likely (contrary to expectations) to be in kinship placements. Various reasons for these differences have been suggested and include contact arrangements precluding adoption; social workers preferring a "same-race" foster placement over a "transracial" adoption; foster carers not having the financial resources to adopt; and a tendency for minority ethnic children to drift in temporary placements (Humphreys *et al*, 1999; Thoburn *et al*, 2005).

Children adopted from care

Minority ethnic children are slightly less likely than white children to be placed for adoption. Statistics from the DCSF (2009) show that, in the year 2008–9, 82 per cent of adopted children were white, 12 per cent of mixed ethnicity, three per cent black, two per cent Asian and one per cent from "other ethnic" groups. These statistics highlight how white and mixed ethnicity children are over-represented in the adoption statistics while all other ethnic groups are under-represented. There has been much speculation about the reasons for this but little evidence. While the USA has a long history of examining ethnic differences in relation to adoption, this has not been the case in the UK. Research findings from the US may not be applicable in the UK due to the very different make-up of the care population, service delivery and the availability in the UK of universal health services, particularly antenatal care.

Children with adoption recommendations

In relation to looked after children who have adoption recommendations, studies have reported complex family backgrounds (Neil, 2000; Selwyn *et al*, 2006) often involving abuse and neglect. A government review of adoption (Performance and Innovation Unit, 2000) found that children who were being placed for adoption were more likely to be female; of white ethnicity; to have entered care at a younger age; and more likely to have come from a background of abuse and neglect than children in the general looked after population.

Minority ethnic children of all ages also appear to be over-represented in those waiting for adoptive families. Information from the Adoption Register (2006) showed that 31 per cent of waiting children were from an ethnic minority and Collier and colleagues (2000) found that 30–50 per cent of the referrals to the *Be My Parent* family-finding service were of minority ethnic children, particularly black boys. It is assumed that social workers use these services for those children who are hardest to place and that, therefore, the ethnic profile of the children reflects the difficulty social workers have in finding new families. There have also been concerns about the disproportionately low numbers of minority ethnic sibling groups referred to the Adoption Register compared to the number of minority ethnic children referred to be placed singly (BAAF, 2007).

Underlying processes

While it is clear that minority ethnic children are over-represented in the care system and under-represented amongst those going forward to adoption, there is little good evidence about the processes that underlie these differences. For example, we do not know how many are diverted away from the adoption pathway before the point where a "should be placed for adoption" recommendation is considered. Moreover, little is known about the care pathways of minority ethnic children or the stability of their placements. Thoburn and colleagues' review (2005) noted that there is very little research in this area, and that what there is tends to describe current practice rather than what actually happens to the children.

Against this background, explanations of the reasons for differences between white children and those of minority ethnicity in the care system and in adoptive placements can only be speculative. Over-representation in the care system may arise through the application of *differential thresholds for placement,* so that minority ethnic children are more easily taken into care or enter care older, and *differential discharge rates* may also lead to an accumulation of longer-stay minority ethnic children in the system as a whole. As the literature suggests that minority ethnic children are taking different pathways through the care system, this study is concerned with the processes generating this difference, the pathways to permanence, the outcomes, and the reasons for what happens to the children. Some of these processes are discussed below.

Delay

We know that there are differential delays in the placement of minority ethnic children in adoptive families (Performance and Innovation Unit,

2000). For example, for all age groups, the process from the adoption recommendation to adoption takes longer for minority ethnic children than it does for white children. Ivaldi (2000) estimated that it takes 200 days longer on average for minority ethnic children to be adopted. However, it is not known why minority ethnic children are subject to such delays, which can have detrimental consequences for psychosocial outcomes and reduces the likelihood of finding an adoptive family (Lowe et al, 2002; Selwyn et al, 2006).

Differential progress towards adoption is further increased if minority ethnic children are already older than white children when they enter the care system. It will also be intensified if decision-making is slower prior to the adoption recommendation decision. This is because of the effects of age on the probability of placement and the possible deterioration of the children's psychosocial functioning during the period of delay. Delay may also divert focus towards solutions to permanency needs other than adoption, especially if matching criteria for non-adoptive placements are less strict.

It is not known whether there are differences between looked after minority ethnic and white children in the rates of physical and learning disabilities or the extent of emotional and behavioural problems. Differences in emotional and behavioural development might arise because of the effects of delay, cultural factors (Cohen et al, 2001) and the age structures of the groups of children, and through any of the processes described above.

Recruitment and preferences of adopters
It is clear that agencies are struggling to find adoptive parents for minority ethnic children. A number of explanations have been proffered (Dutt and Sanyal, 1991; Richards and Ince, 2000; Sunmonu, 2000). These include poor recruitment efforts; social workers' desire to achieve exact matches with the children's heritages; a preference amongst potential minority ethnic carers for foster or kinship care for cultural and/or financial reasons; institutional racism; and differential acceptance of contact arrangements or differences in contact arrangements themselves. Some have argued that there has been a reluctance to actively recruit prospective

adopters in mixed relationships (Banks, 1995). Less attention has been paid to the size of the adult population from which adopters might be recruited, although the data from the census suggest that this is a very important factor (Frazer and Selwyn, 2005).

Differential social work activity

We are not aware of any published studies in the UK that examine how social workers think about, or approach the task of, matching, the criteria they use, or whether their views on the "adoptability" of the child affect the care pathways of minority ethnic children. Avery's study (2000) in New York found that, if the social worker believed the child was "not adoptable", there was very little recruitment activity. It is possible that differential activity may also arise during the planning process, so that planning is less decisive or detailed when the permanency plan is first drawn up (by the four-month review), at subsequent review meetings, and when the placement plan is set out following an adoption recommend-ation or during matching. If these processes occur, they may go along with poorer-quality assessments.

High-quality assessments are essential when choosing placements and when deciding on the appropriate match with foster carers or adopters. Cleaver and Walker's study (2004) of the impact of the Assessment Framework[1] suggested that systematic analysis of information was often poor, that Black children were the least likely to have a core assessment, and that the assessment of environmental influences was the area to which social workers paid least attention. However, we know that schools and communities are important to children (Chahal and Julienne, 1999; Tizard and Phoenix, 2002). It is likely that this is a key area to consider when matching, but we do not know whether much attention is given to the neighbourhoods in which adopters or carers live.

---

[1] *The Framework for the Assessment of Children in Need and their Families* was jointly issued by the Department of Health, the Department for Education and Employment and the Home Office in 2000. The aim was to make transparent the evidence base for the Assessment Framework, thereby assisting professionals in their tasks of analysis, judgement and decision making.

Matching

There is an obvious dilemma for social workers in deciding when the injunction to 'give due consideration to the child's religious persuasion, racial origin and cultural and linguistic background'[2] has to give way to the instruction that 'It is unacceptable for a child to be denied loving adoptive parents solely on the grounds that the child and adopter do not share the same racial or cultural background'.[3]

In other words, there is a balance to be struck between finding the right match and causing unnecessary delay. There is no consistent or agreed principle on how to achieve this balance (Performance and Innovation Unit, 2000), but it has been suggested that reluctance to place minority ethnic children with non ethnically matched families has been a significant factor in delay, to the extent that some children come to be seen as 'un-adoptable' (Hayes, 2003). Anecdotes of extreme examples of matching restrictions are common. BAAF (2003) gave the example of a child where the plan was to find parents who could promote the child's Yemeni, Pakistani and Scottish identity and provide the 24-hour care he needed, presumably because of severe disability.

Given the fierceness of the debate and the vagueness of guidance and definitions, it would not be surprising if social workers were unsure on how specific a match should be before it is acceptable. In practice, we do not know what social workers and Children's Services understand by the terms "ethnicity" and "culture", how they arrive at matching criteria, what flexibility they allow in these, and when and how they decide that a non-matched adoption, usually with white adopters, is the way forward. The importance of religion in matching has also received little research attention, although it is a key issue for many minority ethnic families (Alam and Husband, 2006; Barn et al, 2006; Department for Communities and Local Government, 2006).

Surprisingly, we do not know how many non-matched ("transracial") adoptive placements there are (Ivaldi, 2000). The numbers appeared to be falling, but it is not known whether recent policy and legislation have reversed this trend. Ivaldi (1998) and Thoburn and colleagues (2000)

---

[2]   s. 1 (5) *Adoption and Children Act 2002*
[3]   LAC (1998) *Adoption: Achieving the right balance*, Department of Health

suggest that most of the recent transracial placements have arisen when white English foster carers adopted children they had looked after for many years. Ivaldi's survey in 2000 found that disabled minority ethnic children were three times more likely to be placed with a white carer than non-disabled minority ethnic children. This suggests that the rigidity associated with "same-race" matching policies is not used consistently for all children and even less so for those with special needs. We do not know how social workers and Children's Services arrive at matching criteria, what flexibility they allow in these and how they decide that adoption by white adopters is the way forward. Although debates have begun about the matching process and possible alternative models (Cousins, 2003), ideas on what constitutes best practice arouse strong emotions.

Researchers (Rushton and Minnis, 1997) have accepted the requirement that social workers take ethnicity into account when matching children with adopters, although the evidence they used to support this conclusion was not strong. The two most common arguments are that matching on ethnicity facilitates the development of a positive ethnic/racial identity and that it better prepares children to cope with racism.

These two propositions are potentially researchable, even given the difficulties of deciding and defining what a positive racial/ethnic identity would be, especially for children with mixed heritages. Identity issues are usually thought about in two ways. The first concerns the individual child's comfort with her/his own history and experiences and the self-image and self-esteem the child develops. The second involves a hope and expectation on the part of others that the child will see themselves as part of the culture of their parents, relatives and community. These two views of identity are not necessarily compatible.

Many of the concerns raised by adults focus on the importance of maintaining a sense of ethnic and cultural belonging. This argument is often supported by the view that a failure to develop such an ethnic attachment will lead to identity confusion and mental health issues later in life. There is not a strong body of data on the question either of identity or identity confusion or on the transmission of skills and the ability to confront racism. The evidence that does exist does not decisively support the advantages of matching on ethnicity for these two outcomes (Quinton, 2010).

Of course, research-based assessments of identity may be too crude to pick up advantages that might accrue from matching in promoting a greater degree of comfort with who one is and where one comes from. At present, firm conclusions about matching on ethnicity with respect to these outcomes are not possible. It does seem to be the case, however, that a child and young person's own agency in constructing their identity, especially when their parentage is ethnically mixed, has not been given sufficient weight.

Matching children of mixed ethnic heritage

All these issues concerning identity, cultural and community attachment and matching are brought into sharp focus for children of mixed ethnicity, the largest group of young minority ethnic children in the care system.

Matching children with adopters when both birth parents are of the same ethnicity is, in principle, neither contentious nor problematic, although there may be difficulties because of a shortage of potential adopters. However, when grandparents and/or birth parents are of different ethnicity and perhaps faith too, the difficulties, both conceptual and practical, can become much more formidable. Since the majority of minority ethnic children placed for adoption have mixed parentage – usually of a white mother with a minority ethnic father (Barn, 1993; Barn et al, 1997) – such difficulties are all too common.

The practical difficulties may arise because the ethnicity of the fathers may be unknown, siblings may be of different ethnic mixes, and ethnically-matched adopters may not be available. The conceptual and definitional difficulties arise not only because of the complexities of the issue but also because fierce arguments have arisen about the ethnic status and categorisation of these children. There is an element in this of the principle of categorising people as Black rather than White if they have inherited any "black blood" (Owusu-Bempah, 2005) – a modern use of the United States "one-drop rule"[4] used as a segregating principle in both slavery and apartheid.

---

[4] The "one-drop rule" is a historical colloquial term for a belief among some people in the USA that a person with any trace of African ancestry is Black.

Some writers identify any child who has a minority ethnic parent/ grandparent as Black, because they believe society will view them as such and therefore they need a Black identity and to be in a Black placement to be psychologically healthy (Small, 2000; Maximé, 1993). More positively, others have argued that White and Black children should be placed with minority ethnic families, because they will be provided with the opportunity to benefit from the skills and solidarity of a Black group, to claim Black cultural traditions, and to demonstrate a positive choice to belong to a marginalised group (Prevatt-Goldstein, 2000; Flynn, 2000).

In the arguments about whose heritage the children should be encouraged to feel part of, the predicted ill effects of identity conflicts are particularly prominent. For example, the Chair of the Equality and Human Rights Commission (Phillips, 2007) described mixed ethnicity children as 'being unsure which community they belong to . . . who grow up marooned between two communities . . . falling to "identity stripping"'. Research has not supported the arguments about identity conflict and psychological ill health for those of mixed ethnicity. Rather, most mixed ethnicity children have been shown to grow up with pride and to develop a positive self-image (Wilson, 1987; Katz, 1996; Prevatt-Goldstein, 1999; Tizard and Phoenix, 2002; Harman and Barn, 2005). Indeed, in terms of educational achievement, the 2001 Census demonstrated that 'with the exception of the mixed white and black Caribbean group, the proportion of all the mixed groups with a higher qualification was higher than that of the general population' (Bradford, 2006, p 34).

In addition, the idea that mixed ethnicity children will be accepted by Asian and African-Caribbean communities and benefit from the solidarity of Black cultural traditions has been challenged (Alibhai-Brown and Montague, 1992; Tikly et al, 2004), as has the notion of a single "Black identity" (Modood, 1994). Some sociologists (e.g. Gilroy, 1990; Macey, 1995) are also very critical of a social work tendency to see "ethnicity" and "culture" as fixed and static and believe a policy of "same-race" placements is divisive.

There has been a growth in the view that parents of mixed ethnicity children need to raise their children to recognise *all* their heritages for a healthy identity (Oriti et al, 1996; Wehrly, 2003; Rockquemore and Laszloffy, 2005; Crippen and Brew, 2007). Essentially, "race" remains a focus in these arguments but "mixed" is regarded as a legitimate separate racial identity. Indeed, many writers see the growth of the mixed population as disrupting the old Black/White dichotomy and challenging by cultural ethnic plurality – what Hall has termed the 'new ethnicities' (1992, p 257).

Concluding comments

This review has highlighted the patchiness of the research data on the care pathways of children of minority ethnicity, as well as the very strong opinions and feelings concerning the ways in which Black children and families are treated within the care system. At present, we lack good data and conceptual clarity on children with minority ethnic heritages. These omissions are particularly apparent in the case of children of mixed ethnicities, who form the majority of young children of minority ethnicity in the care system, and around whom the debates about belonging are most passionate.

This study intends to provide a first look at the possible differential progress of minority ethnic children towards permanence and at the processes underlying these pathways, including variations in social work beliefs and practices. We hope that the study will illuminate social work practice in this field and help to fill some of the many gaps in knowledge about the planning and placements of minority ethnic children.

2   Study design and method

This study was commissioned to find out more about the placement plans and moves towards adoption for children of minority ethnicity. The intention was to:

- examine whether social work plans, provision of services and decisions led to disparity in placement plans; and
- examine the decision-making, delays and placement histories for children where adoption was being planned.

Within these broad aims, the following factors that might differentially affect placement pathways were also considered:

- reasons for any delay in decision-making;
- the quality of assessments and planning;
- social workers' considerations and beliefs about matching;
- variations in planning and decision-making for children from different minority ethnic groups and between authorities.

Design

This study drew two retrospective samples (referred to as the *comparison sample* and the *adoption recommended sample*) and one prospective sample (referred to as the *social work interview sample*). These were drawn from three local authorities, one in London, one in the Midlands, and one in the North of England. These three authorities were chosen because of their high and contrasting minority ethnic populations. The retrospective approach was used so that we could collect complete data for the two samples over a defined period. The prospective study was designed to track in real time social workers' thinking and decision-making for children as they moved through the adoption process.

The retrospective samples

The comparison sample of looked after white and minority ethnicity children (n = 102)

The first task was to find out whether white children and children of minority ethnicity had different family and care histories from each other, and the influences these may have on decisions about permanence. To do this, random stratified samples of white and minority ethnic children were drawn. The sample was stratified to make sure that there were sufficient minority ethnic children for the comparison to be meaningful. The intention was to have 55 children in each group. To this end, 110 children aged ten or under, who started to be looked after by the three authorities between 1 April 2002 and 31 March 2003 (excluding those entering on an agreed series of short breaks), were sampled. The upper age limit was applied as only five per cent of children are adopted over the age of ten (DCSF, 2008).

When children's files were later read, four children had been incorrectly entered on their authorities' database as white, when they were of mixed ethnicity. A further four children's files could not be located and had to be excluded. Therefore, the final comparison sample was of 48 white children and 54 children from a minority ethnic background: a final overall sample of 102 children. Data collection on these children began in January 2005 and finished in August 2005.

This sample was intended to answer questions about differences between white and minority ethnic children in their characteristics, entry to care, service use, decision-making, and placement outcomes.

The sample of minority ethnic children with an adoption recommendation (n = 120)

We wanted to learn more about the differences there might be between black, Asian and mixed ethnicity children in their characteristics and how decisions about them were taken forward once a panel had recommended that they be placed for adoption. A second complete sample was therefore drawn across the three authorities of all the minority ethnic children who had a recommendation for adoption (n = 120) made between 1 April 2005 and 31 March 2006. Data collection began in July 2005 and finished in January 2007.

The social work interview sample (n = 49)

The purpose of this part of the study was to follow the adoption decision-making process in real time through interviews with the children's social workers. This was done to ensure that the detail and complexity of each case was captured, something that is very hard to retrieve from children's files. To compile this sample, the professional advisers to the adoption panel were contacted monthly from November 2005 to December 2007, and asked to identify minority ethnic children due to be considered by the adoption panel. One child from each sibling group was randomly selected to ensure that the findings would not be influenced by a social worker who happened to be dealing with a large sibling group, and so that the variation in social workers' views and in the children's ethnicities were maximised. We naturally wanted to collect a sample of all the minority ethnic children who were being considered by the adoption panel. However, one social worker refused to be interviewed about two of her cases and another case was missed because of late notification by a professional adviser.

The number of children's cases going to panel was lower than expected. The introduction of the Adoption and Children Act (2002) and the need for Placement Orders meant that some workers and legal departments were unsure about how to take adoption cases forward. There was also confusion within the local authorities on whether it was possible to promote children without a Placement Order. For this reason, the number of children going to the panel for an adoption recommendation was reduced. By the end of 2007, we had a sample of 50 minority ethnic children and 49 social workers (one social worker was responsible for two of the children). All the children's files were read and data collected in the same way as in the other samples.

Final sample numbers

It is important to recognise that the intention of this study was to maximise available data by choosing representative samples, and to open up an area that is contested, but about which there is very little systematic research. Two methodological consequences of the sampling strategy should be noted. First, that 13 minority ethnic children who were in the comparison sample also appear in the adoption recommended sample, because they happened to have adoption recommendations within the sampling periods. Secondly, interviews with social workers took place in the week before the panel was due to consider the adoption recommendation, and sometimes events occurred which meant the adoption recommendation was not made. However, these children were not excluded as we were interested in why panel bookings did not progress, and we continued to make monthly follow-up calls to social workers to track the children's progress.

Table 2.1
The final samples by ethnicity and the number of sibling groups

	Minority ethnic children	White children	Sibling groups
Comparison	54	48	10
Adoption recommended	120	0	16
Social work interview	50	0	0

Table 2.2
The final samples by authority

	North	Midlands	London
Comparison	43	14	45
Adoption recommended	40	36	44
Social work interview	26	9	15

The local authorities were specifically selected because of their high and contrasting minority populations and therefore comparison with national data on looked after children are not relevant. The Northern authority had a high Pakistani population, the Midlands a high African-Caribbean and mixed ethnicity populations and the London borough a high Bangladeshi population.

Data collection

The case files of all the children were read and data collected in the same way for each sample.

Case file data

Previous work on the study, *Costs and Outcomes of Non-Infant Adoptions* (Selwyn *et al*, 2006), the Integrated Children's System and the 2001 Census informed the development of the case file schedules. A coding manual with clear rating criteria accompanied the schedule. The first section included information on the characteristics of the child and the backgrounds of the parents. The child's care pathway was divided into three stages relating to key decision-making points. The three stages were:

Stage 1: Child supported in the family

This covered the period from the child's first referral to Children's Services to the point at which they were looked after for more than six weeks. This first period of six weeks was chosen because of the well-known findings from the "leaving care curve" on the diminished pro-bability of return home after this time. Data were collected on referrals, services to support the family, assessments, factors influencing delay, and the psychosocial outcomes of the children.

Stage 2: Child looked after

This stage started from the point when the child was first looked after for more than six weeks to:

a) the date of the adoption panel or
b) the date the child was returned home or
c) the date that the file was examined in cases where the child was still looked after without an adoption recommendation.

Data were collected on the reasons for admission, placements, assessments, plans, delays, services, contact with birth parents and child outcomes.

Stage 3: Adoption recommendation
This stage was only completed for children who had had an adoption recommendation made by a panel. Data were collected on plans, services, matching requirements, adoption processes, placements, and child outcomes.

Collecting data on ethnicity, language, culture and religion

A framework was developed to ensure that attention was paid to culture, language, and identity, religion and ethnicity at all stages of the study. During the data collection, we were looking at how these were described, in what sort of contexts "differences" were discussed, what meanings were given to perceived "differences" and what action or inaction resulted. These data were recorded verbatim from case file records and we also noted when nothing was recorded. Our framework informed every element of the data collection.

Developing the prospective study interview schedules

An interview schedule was prepared drawing on the literature and the knowledge and experience of members of the professionals' advisory and two service user groups. The service user groups were self-selected and composed mainly of older children who were already active within their authority's partnership and leaving care groups. We had two successful group-work meetings, one in the North and the other in the London borough.

Face-to-face interviews with social workers

Each social worker was interviewed at work with interviews lasting about an hour. The interviews focused on how social workers identified the child's needs, their approach to matching and family finding, how they grappled with difficult matching decisions, and their views on timescales and the new legislation. The final interview schedule included some pre-coded questions, as well as open text replies. Interviews were arranged with the child's social worker before the social worker attended the adoption panel, so that any concerns about panel and changes of plan could be tracked later.

Follow-up telephone interviews

The first follow-up telephone interview was conducted as soon as possible after the panel had met. Thereafter, social workers were telephoned monthly to check on progress and for any changes in the plan. No more calls were made once the child was placed. This process was useful, as it revealed the cases where social workers had changed, where plans had changed, or where social workers were absent because of long-term sickness. One final call was made in July/August 2007 to check the whereabouts of all the 50 children.

Data analysis

Data from children's files were entered on an Access database and analysed within Access, SPSS and STATA. The qualitative data from files were entered in NVivo and coded up from the data. All face-to-face interviews were tape recorded and transcribed for analysis. The interview data were coded by hand and in NVivo. This was done because not all of the team had training in the use of NVivo, but primarily it was a check on the categories and codes that we had created as a research team, which included white and minority ethnic researchers. The qualitative data were used to illustrate and give a deeper understanding of the numerical analysis of pre-coded questions.

In this book, we have chosen to use extracts from case files and interviews without making any grammatical changes, to retain the nuances and credibility of the data. Very occasionally, a word has been added to extracts to clarify the meaning.

Final comment on the methodology

- The study design and sample selection were selected to open up a poorly researched field. We needed adequate numbers of children of minority ethnicity and so we chose three local authorities with high and contrasting minority ethnic populations. This strategy naturally has an impact on the generalisations that can be made/conclusions that can be drawn from the study. Policy and practice may be different in local authorities that have smaller minority ethnic populations, or indeed, in others with higher minority ethnic populations.

- The majority of all the minority ethnic children in the three samples were of mixed ethnicity. The low numbers of Asian and especially black children, together with the complication of sibling groups, limit the ability to generalise from the findings for them.
- Finally, most of the data came from children's case files and more services may have been provided than were recorded.

For all these reasons, this study should be seen as the beginning of research on issues of permanence for children of minority ethnicity, not an answer to all we might want to know.

3   The comparison sample: the children and their birth families

This chapter describes the characteristics of the 102 children in the comparison sample, their families, and the involvement of Children's Services and other agencies before the children became looked after. The data are presented as a comparison between minority ethnic and white children, since this reflects the stratification of the sample.

The children's characteristics

The sample comprised 102 looked after children of whom 53 per cent were from a minority ethnic background and 47 per cent were white. There were slightly more boys than girls and this reflected the numbers in the whole cohort of children that this sample was drawn from.

Table 3.1
The gender and ethnicity of the children

	Minority ethnic children *(n = 54)*	*White children* *(n = 48)*
Boys	29 (54%)	25 (52%)
Girls	25 (46%)	23 (48%)

Siblings

Efforts to ensure that the sample did not include any large sibling groups were thwarted by children having different surnames, and relationships that only became apparent after reading the children's files. In all, there were ten sibling groups: seven pairs, one set of twins and two groups of four siblings. Therefore, the 102 children came from 88 families. One group of siblings was of African-Caribbean ethnicity and because there were only seven children of black ethnicity in the sample, these four siblings had a major impact on analysis of this ethnic category.

There was little difference in the birth positions of children of white and minority ethnicity, with the majority (67%) not being the first-born child. Most (56%) came from large families and had more than three siblings: 21 per cent had between five and nine siblings and one child had 18 full siblings. Just over half (51%) of those with brothers and sisters had at least one sibling on the Child Protection Register and about a quarter (26%) had a brother or sister of an ethnicity different to their own.

The children's nationality and ethnicity

Nearly all (98%) of the children in the sample were British citizens except for one German and one black African child who was an asylum seeker. The ethnicity of the children was often complex. Table 3.2 places the children within ethnic categories, as defined by the Census, but these categories are limited and are only based on what was known about the parents' ethnicity.

Table 3.2
The children's ethnicity as recorded on the children's files

	Ethnicity	Number of children	Sub-group totals
WHITE CHILDREN n = 48			
White	White	45	100%
	White Other	2	
	White Irish	1	
MINORITY ETHNIC CHILDREN n = 54			
Mixed ethnicity	White/Asian	15	57%
	White/Black Caribbean	9	
	Mixed other	4	
	White/Black African	3	
Asian	Pakistani	7	30%
	Bangladeshi	5	
	Indian	3	
	Asian other	1	
Black	Black Caribbean	6	13%
	Black African	1	

In Table 3.2, we can see that the minority ethnic children in this sample came from many different ethnic backgrounds. The majority (57%) of the mixed ethnicity children had Asian fathers. The category "mixed other" was used to describe a wide range of ethnic mixes: Vietnamese/white British, Kosovan/white British, African/Caribbean, and Chinese/white British.

The children's religion

Whether or not the child had a religion was recorded on 79 per cent of children's files. There was no information for nine per cent of the children of minority ethnicity and 27 per cent of the white children. The majority of children were of Christian faith, with "no religion" being the next most common description. Thirty-six per cent of those whose faith was recorded as Muslim were of mixed ethnicity.

Table 3.3
The children's religion as recorded on the children's files

Religion	Minority ethnic children (n = 46)	White children (n = 35)
No religion	12	15
Christian	11	19
Muslim	22	0
Hindu	1	0
Mormon	0	1

Religious affinities were not as frequently documented as ethnicity and only "Christian" faiths were further differentiated by branch. For example, "Christian" was followed by "Roman Catholic" or "Anglican" or "Episcopal". Other religions had no other descriptions added so, for example, Sunni and Shia Muslims were not distinguished. This may reflect social workers' greater awareness of the differences between Christian religious groups and/or alternatively, other religious groups in the UK may have fewer divisions.

The children's language

English was the first language of the majority (81%) of the children and the language spoken at home. The first language for a few children was Bengali/Sylheti, Punjabi, Gujerati, Spanish or Lingala. Seven per cent of the children were bilingual, speaking English and at least one other language.

The birth parents

There were incomplete data on the children's parents. As there were ten sibling groups within this sample of 102 children, there were 88 birth mothers and probably 90 fathers. There were minimal data on 25 of these fathers and incomplete information on the remainder. Four mothers and one father of minority ethnic children had died before the family was referred to Children's Services, as had two fathers of white children. The majority of these early deaths were the consequence of drug misuse.

The parents' nationality and ethnicity

Most parents were British citizens: 89 per cent of the birth mothers and 91 per cent of the known birth fathers. Three fathers were seeking asylum. There was insufficient information on children's files to be certain about whether parents were the first, second or third generation to live in the UK. It appeared that over half (58%) of the minority ethnic birth mothers had been born elsewhere, as had 40 per cent of the minority ethnic birth fathers. In only eleven cases was there information about when and how the child's birth parents had arrived in the UK and just two detailed descriptions of how parents had experienced this dislocation: one a boat refugee from Vietnam and the other fleeing from war in Kosovo. However, only eight children had *both* parents born outside the UK and most of these had come from Pakistan.

In a few cases, descriptions of parental ethnicity changed in the files. Sometimes it appeared that a new social worker had incorrectly noted the ethnicity. Once recorded incorrectly, it tended to stay uncorrected. Parents also sometimes chose to define their ethnicity differently. In the following extract, from a social worker's recording, a mixed ethnicity mother, who had never known her own Asian father and had grown up with her white English mother, decided to change her name:

Birth mother has changed her name [both first and second] and it is believed this is an attempt to identify with her own father's ethnic background. She does not personally practise as a Muslim and was not brought up as a Muslim. Religion would seem to be an expression of her own identity issues rather than her religion. This would be an issue in matching and ideally a family would have to be found that could embrace all the cultural issues.

There were other examples where it was not possible to explain why there were so many changes. For example, in one case a child's father was initially described as Asian but the recording then changed to White/Asian. By the time the Care Order was being heard, he was described by the social worker as Ugandan Asian but by the guardian as a Black Indian/Kenyan.

The majority of birth mothers (n = 71) were white English and this, of course, was partly because of the sampling strategy. However, within the minority ethnic children's group, 23 of the children's mothers were also white. Nearly all the mixed ethnicity children had a white English mother and a minority ethnic father. The table below describes the ethnicity of the 54 minority ethnic children's parents and their partnerships, as recorded on files.

Table 3.4
The ethnic partnerships of minority ethnic children's parents

Ethnicity of mother	White father	Black father	Asian father	Mixed ethnicity father	Kosovan father	Missing data
White (n = 23)		6	12	3	1	1
Asian (n = 15)			15			
Black (n = 9)	1	7				1
Mixed ethnicity (n = 6)	1	2	2	1		
Vietnamese (n = 1)	1					

The white mothers in this sample had mainly had relationships with Pakistani men. The other mixed relationships were three white mothers/ African-Caribbean fathers, two white mothers/Bangladeshi fathers and two white mothers/black African fathers and one white mother/black "other ethnicity" father.

Mother's language

Many of the minority ethnic children's mothers were white English and therefore were English speakers. There were 11 mothers who could not speak English and most were from the Indian sub-continent. Six children lived in a family where neither parent spoke English.

Religion

Religion was not recorded for 27 of children's mothers and this was more frequently the case when the mother was white. White mothers were recorded as being Christian (31), having no religion (21), Muslim (2) and Mormon (1), whereas the minority ethnic mothers were Muslim (13), had no religion (5), were Hindu (1) and Christian (1). There were too many missing data on fathers to give informative percentages, but their recorded religions followed the same pattern as the mothers, with the majority of white fathers being Christian and minority ethnic fathers Muslim.

Mother's age

At the time the children first became looked after, the children's mothers were on average[5] 28 years old (range 15–49 years old) and fathers on average aged 30 (range 18–47 years old). The mothers and fathers of the minority ethnic children tended to be slightly older than the parents of white children.

Households

At the time of the referral to Children's Services, just under half (46%) of all the children were being cared for by both parents. This was especially the case for the majority (75%) of Asian children. In comparison, most

---

[5] average = mean

black and mixed ethnicity children were living only with their mother; fathers were often absent. Male boyfriends/partners were living in some of the households but their presence was often fleeting.

Some children had other living arrangements at the time of the referral. Three children were living with single carers from their extended family and another child had been abandoned. A quarter of the mothers (16% minority ethnic and 9% white) shared their homes with other adults such as grandparents, aunts, uncles and family friends. Information on children's files did not provide enough detail to know whether the birth parents were gaining support from the additional adults, or whether these adults also needed care.

Extended family support
Over half (57%) of the children's families had some helpful contact with extended family members. Minority ethnic children were nearly three times less likely[6] to get support from extended family members than white children. However, there were significant differences *within* the minority ethnic group with mixed ethnicity children's families having the least support of all.[7] The Asian children's families had similar levels of support to the white families, while support of black families resembled that of the mixed ethnicity families. The vulnerability of these families, within the child welfare context, deserves greater attention when planning services for children in need. Where relatives did provide support, it was mainly children's grandparents who came to the aid of white mothers and aunts and uncles for minority ethnic mothers.

Family histories
There were gaps in information about the histories of the parents on files, especially the fathers, often because the parent had refused to give the information or the information was not known. More white than minority ethnic mothers had spent time in the care system and had had previous

---

[6] chi-square = (1), 5.149, p<.023 odds ratio 2.8
[7] Mixed ethnicity children had significantly less support from extended family than white children p<.005, r = -0.3

contact with the local authority about the quality of their care of other children. Therefore, assessments had been completed and Children's Services knew more about the families of the white children at the time the sample child was referred.

Table 3.5
Risk factors in maternal histories

	Minority ethnic mothers (n = 31)	White mothers with minority ethnic children (n = 23)	White mothers with white children (n = 48)
	%	%	%
Victim of childhood abuse/neglect	26	83	23
Period in care during childhood	16	52	54
History of maternal violent behaviour	16	30	13
Known history of abuse to children	13	26	17
Served a prison sentence	6	13	13

Referrals

At the time the children were born, Children's Services were already working with 42 per cent of their families. For a further ten per cent, the birth of the child triggered the re-opening of a closed case. New referrals were received for 49 children (50% of the minority ethnic children and 46% of the white children), and a small number of these were before the birth of the child. More white than minority ethnic children were referred by community child health services but the difference did not reach statistical significance. Eighteen per cent of children had had previous referrals (range 2–5 previous referrals) before the key referral that began sustained Children's Services involvement. In this study we have taken all measures of time and children's age from the date of the key referral.

Children's age at referral

Statistically, there was no difference in the age of minority ethnic children and white children at referral: the majority (79%) were under a year old, 15 per cent were aged between one and four years and six per cent between five and seven years. However, there was one difference within the groups, with black children being older on average than the other groups and having a wider age spread (Fig 3.1). This may have been a consequence of the large sibling group in this sample.

Figure 3.1
Children's ages in weeks at the beginning of Children's Services involvement

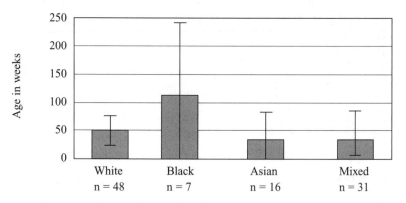

Reasons for referral

The most common reasons (58%) for referral were concerns about abuse and neglect. More white children (42%) were referred for reasons of neglect than minority ethnic children (32%), but more minority ethnic children (30%) than white children (25%) were referred because of concerns about abuse. However, the difference was not statistically significant. When the ethnicity of the mother was examined, children of white mothers were significantly more likely to be referred for neglect[8] (see Table 3.6).

Table 3.6
Primary reason for referral by ethnicity

	Minority ethnic children n = 54 %	White children n = 48 %
Neglect	32	42
Abuse	30	25
Family in acute stress/ potential abuse	17	6
Family dysfunction	9	11
Parental illness/disability	7	6
Parental request for adoption	5	4
Absent parenting	0	6

Agencies working with the children's families at the time of the referral

Many families had other agencies working with them: just five families had only Children's Services involved. Community child health services such as health visitors and GPs were working with many families (55%) and other services such as the probation service (12%), family centres (9%), and adult mental health (8%) and drug/alcohol services (8%) were also involved. There were no statistically significant differences between the minority ethnic children and white children on which agencies were involved with their families.

---

[8]   Fisher's Exact, p = 0.023: 44 per cent of children with white mothers and 19 per cent of children with minority ethnic mothers were referred because of concerns about neglect.

Child Protection Register
The reason for referral was also reflected in the categories under which the children were later registered on the Child Protection Register. More white children were registered overall (60% white children compared to 50% minority ethnicity children) and more of the white children were registered for neglect (46% white compared to 28% minority ethnicity). In this sample, the proportion of mixed ethnicity children registered (61%) was similar to that of the white group. There were few registrations of Asian or black children.

Thirty per cent of children became looked after within a month of Children's Services involvement: many of these within a few days of birth. The plan for the majority of the families was to ascertain whether parents could adequately care for their children and to provide support to enable children to remain at home. There was little difference between the ethnic groups as to whether referrals were made to other family support agencies such as family centres. A somewhat higher proportion of white children were referred to other agencies for non-residential support (33% white compared to 22% minority ethnicity), but this difference was not statistically significant.

Social work assessments began as soon as the key referral was received. The following chapter describes the information that was collected on families and the services provided.

Summary

- The sample comprised 48 white and 54 minority ethnic children from 88 families.
- Fifty-seven per cent of the minority ethnic children were of mixed ethnicity, 30 per cent were Asian and 13 per cent black. Fifty per cent of the minority ethnic children had a white mother.
- The majority of children (67%) were not the first born, and just over a quarter (26%) of those with siblings had a brother or sister with a different ethnicity.
- Most birth parents had been born in the UK. Nineteen per cent of birth mothers and 17 per cent of birth fathers had been born elsewhere but just eight children had both parents who were first generation

immigrants. There was very little information on files about the circumstances that brought the parents to the UK or the impact of dislocation.

- In comparison with minority ethnic mothers, more white mothers had suffered abuse and neglect in their own childhood and more had spent time in care.
- Forty-two per cent of children's families were already involved with Children's Services at the time of the referral of the sample child. The vast majority of families were also involved with other agencies.
- About half the children's families (52%) had support from relatives. Minority ethnic families, particularly mixed ethnicity families, were nearly three times as likely not to have extended family support in comparison with white families.
- The children of white mothers were more likely to be referred for neglect than the children of minority ethnic mothers.
- The majority (77%) of children were under a year old when referred to Children's Services. More black children were older at referral.

4 Assessment, support and decisions

We assembled information from all the social work assessments on the children's files, to provide a picture of the birth families. It was often not possible to determine whether there had been an initial assessment, as assessments were rarely labelled in this way. Similarly, "core assessments" were often not based on the "triangle" in the Assessment Framework[9] and some were not dated but there was often a whole range of other assessments on file, such as risk and comprehensive assessments. Over a third (38%) of all children did not have a recognisable core or comprehensive assessment on file and seven (11%) of the 63 core assessments were incomplete. Forty-four per cent of white children and 33 per cent of minority ethnic children did not have a core assessment. This difference between groups was not statistically significant.

Core assessments were usually begun on children and their families whilst children were still living at home and more than half (59%) of them were linked to Care Order applications. A few (8) were completed whilst the child was looked after and not involved in court proceedings and five when adoption was being planned for the child.

Agencies contributing to assessments

We were interested in whether other agencies had contributed information to social workers' assessments (see Table 4.1).

Overall, health visitors and GPs contributed to 68 per cent of the assessments and contributed more frequently to the assessment of white children than the assessments of minority ethnic children. Family centres were also involved and contributed to over a third (35%) of all assessments. "Other agencies" also contributed to about a third of assessments; this category of "other" contained a variety of agencies each contributing

---

[9]   Information on the Assessment Framework can be found at http://www.dcsf.gov.uk/every childmatters/safeguardingandsocialcare/integratedchildrenssystem/ics/

Table 4.1
Agencies contributing to assessments of children and families

	Minority ethnic children (n = 54) %	White children (n = 48) %
Health visitor	41	50
"Other" agencies	26	48
Family centre/Sure Start	37	54
GP	19	27
CAMHS	15	15
Nursery/School	15	13
Adult mental health	11	8
Probation	4	4

small proportions to the assessment, including agencies such as residential mother and baby units, housing officers, contact supervisors, foster carers and the police. There was no statistical difference between children of minority ethnicity and white children in agencies contributing to the assessments.

Concerns identified and services provided

The assessment process revealed a number of concerns about the care of the children. Not all concerns were evidenced, and therefore we also recorded when there were strong suspicions that adverse parental behaviours were occurring. The following analysis has been conducted broadly to examine differences between the parents of the white and minority ethnic children. Differences within the minority ethnic group will be examined in Chapter 8 with a larger minority ethnic sample.

Parenting capacity

Domestic violence was the most common parenting concern (see Table 4.2) and just over half of the families experiencing domestic violence also had a parent involved in criminal behaviour. Although domestic violence was suspected or evidenced in 63 per cent of families, there were few recorded interventions designed to tackle the abuse: only two white mothers used a women's refuge.

Table 4.2
Parental behaviours of concern

	Minority ethnic children's parents (n = 54) %	White children's parents (n = 48) %
Domestic violence	63	63
Substance misuse	52	41
Alcohol misuse	30	53
Criminal involvement/prison	54	42

There were also high levels of drug and alcohol misuse. White children's parents had higher levels of alcohol misuse than parents of minority ethnic children and it was also mainly white mothers who were misusing drugs. However, only 12 per cent of children's parents took up specialist drug/alcohol services. In all cases where support was provided, parents were thought to be misusing drugs *and* alcohol.

Abuse
This dimension was not assessed by social workers in two cases: one where the assessment occurred pre-birth and another where the parents refused to co-operate. The following accounts of abuse are taken from the assessment documents on the children's files. Thirteen children were removed at birth and were therefore not subject to abuse.

Abandonment and rejection

Forty-four per cent of the children experienced some rejection by their birth parents with five children being singled out for rejection. Eighteen children (13 children of minority ethnicity and five white children) had been abandoned: 13 on one occasion and five children more than once (range 2–5 times). Of the 13 abandoned minority ethnic children, nine were of mixed ethnicity.

Table 4.3
Number and types of abuse experienced by children

	Minority ethnic children (n = 53)*	White children (n = 47)*
	%	%
Four types of abuse (neglect, physical, sexual and emotional abuse)	4	11
Three types of abuse (neglect, physical and emotional abuse)	15	21
Two types of abuse	38	17
One type of abuse	40	28
No abuse or neglect	4	25

* *Note*: this dimension was not assessed in two cases, which explains the decrease in numbers.

Neglect

Seventy of the children were neglected. The majority of these children experienced gross global neglect with 13 of the children experiencing intermittent neglect. There were no statistical differences by ethnicity.

Sexual abuse

Very few children were known to have been sexually abused: three minority ethnicity children and six white children. Most of the abuse was thought to be inappropriate touching although two children were also subjected to penetrative sex. Three fathers, two extended family members, a sibling, and a stranger had committed the abuse. In two cases, the abuser was unknown.

Physical abuse
Thirty-three children were physically abused (30% minority ethnicity and 35% white children) with about 10 per cent suffering broken bones and/or burns.

Emotional abuse
Thirty-four children were emotionally abused (31% minority ethnicity and 35% white children). Most of this emotional abuse took the form of persistent humiliation and belittlement. Nine parents involved their children in criminal activities (three minority ethnicity and six white children), and eight children (four minority ethnic and four white children) were terrorised by parental threats of being left alone or being sent away.

Multiple abuse
Just over half the children experienced more than one form of abuse. Neglect was the most common type of abuse where only one was described.

Family and environmental factors which may have an impact on the capacity to parent

This area of children's lives was poorly assessed. Fourteen per cent of assessments had no mention of this dimension and the remainder had very little information. Seven children had experienced the death of a parent, and other parents had arrived in the UK as refugees, but the impact of loss and dislocation on family functioning were rarely discussed.

Harassment and racism
There was little recorded about experiences of racial harassment (two cases), and it was not clear whether this was because it was not occurring or because these experiences had not been asked about or recorded. Previous research (Chahal and Julienne, 1999; Gray, 2002) has highlighted the discrimination and frequent racial abuse experienced by many minority ethnic families.

There was slightly more information about other kinds of harassment with 19 per cent of white and nine per cent of minority ethnic children's families facing harassment such as being bullied by neighbours and sometimes by extended family members. Examples of harassment included being pestered by drug dealers or harassed by family members because of mental health problems or because of having a mixed ethnicity child. In one case, a single Asian mother was fearful of leaving the house because of attitudes to single parents in her Bangladeshi community.

Community isolation

A third of files contained no data about the family's social and community integration. Where there were data, 35 per cent of families were described as very isolated and there were no statistical differences between white and minority ethnic families. Some mothers had extended family members living nearby but did not feel able to ask for support, and others had contact with relatives who were undermining and occasionally controlling and violent. The following extract from a psychologist's court report is an example of an Asian mother whose contact with her in-laws was very difficult:

> *The reported poor relationship between mother and her in-laws seems to have a strong cultural element to it, i.e. mother's abilities may not have matched her in-laws' expectations and hence she was at the receiving end of severe criticism and hostility, which has further undermined her already compromised abilities and led to further loss of ability to parent her children.*

Housing and debt

Most families (64%) lived in privately rented or social housing, with about 13 per cent at risk of imminent eviction. One white child was from a travelling background. Most of the homes (63%) were described as in poor condition with few toys or books available.

There was no information on half the files about the family's finances. Nine (two minority ethnicity families and seven white children's families) were described as being heavily in debt, but it would be surprising if this was a complete picture of families' finances.

The children's health and development whilst they were living at home

Recording in files suggested that the majority of children were generally in good health with no observable health problems. The greatest area of concern was the impact of exposure to drugs/alcohol in-utero, with 25 per cent of children (19 of minority ethnicity and seven white children) described as either displaying neo-natal abstinence syndrome,[10] or signs of foetal alcohol spectrum disorder (FASD), shortly after birth. The long-term impact on the children's development was as yet unknown.

Thirty-one children became looked after within a month of the referral, and therefore they have been excluded from the next section that describes the educational progress, mental health and development of children while they were living at home.

Education (n = 71)

Most (70%) of the children were below school age, 21 per cent were in mainstream education and nine per cent were attending nursery or playgroups. Only one white child had a statement of special educational needs and educational concerns were recorded for two mixed ethnicity children – one due to truancy and the other due to exclusions. Fifteen per cent of children had language and speech delays.

Mental health and relationships (n = 71)

Many of the children were still very young but 21 per cent were already showing signs of mental ill-health while living at home. Seventeen per cent of these children were displaying behaviours associated with conduct disorder and were reported as being hyperactive. A few (6) had physically harmed someone else and two (both white) were also self-harming. Twenty per cent had some difficulties recorded in their peer relationships and in the quality of their attachment to their main carer.

---

[10] Neo-natal abstinence syndrome as a result of the mother's dependence on drugs during pregnancy. Withdrawal or abstinence symptoms usually develop shortly after birth. Symptoms exhibited are loud, high-pitched crying, sweating, yawning and gastro-intestinal disturbances.

Identity (n = 71)

To examine this area of child development, we selected questions from the section on identity in the Integrated Children's System, such as whether the child attended a place of worship, had dietary needs or took part in cultural activities, and we looked for this information on children's files. There was a dearth of information on identity issues with only five children (four of minority ethnicity and one white child) having anything recorded about this aspect of their lives.

Family support services

All the children's families received social work support. In addition, social workers made 43 referrals to family centres for further assessment. No black families attended a family centre, but 11 white, nine Asian and 11 mixed ethnicity children's families did so. The families did not receive a great deal of support from other agencies. Very few parents and children (four families: two minority ethnic and two white) received therapeutic support from CAMHS – perhaps there were few referrals because of the young age of most of the children. However, many parents also refused proffered services. While the children were being supported in their families, 16 per cent of children's families (11% minority ethnicity and 20% of white children's parents) refused a service and this was often a drug/alcohol service.

Strengths identified in the parent–child relationship

There was nearly an even split with half of the children's families having no identified strengths in the child–parent relationship and half having positive aspects identified in the social work recording such as in the following examples:

> *[Mum] has provided a number of opportunities to play and interact with other children by taking him to a range of mother and toddler groups . . . She has actively encouraged her son to read books.* (Social worker's notes)

[Father] was relaxed and confident whilst handling the child. (Social worker's notes)

There were no differences between ethnicities in relation to whether strengths were identified or not.

Parents' comments on the assessment/plan

Over half (54%) the files had recording on the parent's views about the assessment and subsequent plans. We were not able to confirm whether all parents had been asked their views, as we were reliant on social work recording. Three-quarters of parents, whose views were recorded, disagreed with the assessment. There were no differences between ethnicities either in the likelihood of having parental views recorded or in disagreeing with the findings of the assessments.

Placements and moves while children were supported in the family

Although children were living primarily with their birth families, some also had had short periods of care provided by relatives or family friends. Eighteen per cent were cared for by relatives and 16 per cent had a few days or weeks in short break care. There were no statistical differences in the number of primary carers or placement moves by ethnicity.

Delays in removing the child from the birth family

Delay was defined by the researchers for this period as a lack of movement or change of plan where a child had been supported in their family for a year and there had been no or insufficient improvement. From the evidence on files, it appeared that most children (78%) became looked after at an appropriate time and their social workers had acted promptly in response to increasing concerns. There was no significant difference between the proportions of white and minority ethnic children experiencing delayed intervention.

Table 4.4
Delayed removal from home and the ethnicity of children

	Minority ethnic children *(n = 54)* %	*White children* *(n = 48)* %
No delay	80	77
Delay	20	23

Reasons for delay

From the available evidence, the delay in the child becoming looked after was caused by parental, professional and organisational factors. Nearly half of the children where delay was identified had parents who had refused the offer of support services and perhaps this made them less visible. Thirty per cent of parents also gave the appearance of complying with written agreements, but in reality were not doing so. For example, some mothers said that their violent partner had left when this was not the case. The lack of a social work assessment featured in the cases of 17 per cent of minority ethnic children and six per cent of white children and without an assessment there was often insufficient evidence that thresholds had been reached. Other factors contributing to delay were strong opposition from kin and parents to social work plans (27%), families moving (23%) and staff shortages (14%). In most cases, there were multiple factors influencing the delay in removing the child and those who experienced delay became looked after two to seven years after the referral.

However, the majority of children became looked after quickly: 30 per cent within a month of the referral and a further 33 per cent within the year. Once in care, plans needed to be made about the children's futures. The next chapter considers social work decision-making and placements while the children were looked after.

Summary

- There were no statistical differences between the white and minority ethnic children's families on many measures.
- Core assessments were missing for over a third of children.
- Domestic violence was prevalent in many families and neglect was frequently reported. White parents had more alcohol and drug misuse problems than minority ethnicity parents.
- Just fewer than half the families received support from a family centre but few services from other agencies, partly because of the parent's refusal to accept or attend services that were offered.
- Thirty-seven per cent of the children had a change of primary carer and home before becoming looked after.
- Although most children were still very young, 21 per cent showed signs of mental ill-health while living with their birth families. Twenty-five per cent had been born with symptoms of FASD or neo-natal abstinence syndrome.
- There was a dearth of information on children's files about parental experience of dislocation, experience of harassment and racism, the family's culture or the children's identity needs.
- Thirty per cent of children became looked after within a month of the key referral and an additional 33 per cent within the year.

5   Being looked after

The children in the comparison sample became looked after in the year 1 April 2002–31 March 2003, at the point when family support services had not been successful in keeping the family together. Of course, since the sample only selected looked after children, this failure is not a comment on the success of family support services generally. Data were collected on placements, the extent of contact, and the plans made for the children once they became looked after.

Becoming looked after

Most children became looked after because of increasing risk of significant harm. Emergency powers were used for 42 children: 31 Police Protection Orders and 11 Emergency Protection Orders. These were obtained on average 20 months (range 2–46 months) after Children's Services became involved with the family. For three children an internal local authority audit led to action that brought the child into care.

Age when the children became looked after

The majority of children (66%) became looked after within a year of the referral. There was little difference between the whole minority ethnic group and white children in relation to this. However, as black children were referred at older ages, they were also older on average than other ethnic groups when they became looked after. There were also older children in each of the ethnic groups, as shown in the figure below.

Searching for a kinship carer

Social workers made strenuous efforts to find extended family members and to assess whether there were any kin who could care for the child. It was clear from the files that social workers believed that, wherever possible, extended family members were the best option for children unable to live with their birth parents. Kinship care was promoted because

Figure 5.1
Children's average age in months when first looked after

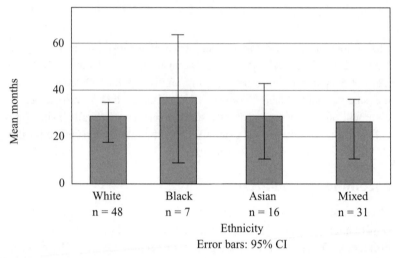

it was thought that kin would provide the link to the child's cultural heritage, be supportive of contact with birth parents, and help the child to understand their identity. It was also important to show in the court arena that all other avenues had been exhausted before planning for other forms of care.

Social workers assessed the relatives of 70 per cent of the minority ethnic children and 48 per cent of white children. Family group conferences were occasionally used. The minutes from conferences suggested that the perceived stigma of care was felt more by minority ethnic families and this sometimes led to pressure on relatives to offer a home. The extract below is taken from the social worker's recording of a family group conference concerning an Asian child:

Mrs X [grandfather's daughter] was clear that she was married, had two young children and was not in a position to care permanently for the children. Mrs X and her father nominated Y [grandfather's eldest son] but he certainly did not nominate himself. The family were invited to talk about it further and let me know of any decision.

Several kin came forward (usually one after the other) asking to be considered as carers for fourteen children. Sometimes this delayed plans for a child, as can be seen in the example below involving another Asian child and her sibling.

Illustrative example

A baby was born in early 2003 to drug-misusing parents and remained in hospital for a month because of heroin withdrawal before being fostered. At a planning meeting the mother stated that she wanted her sister to care for the baby, but during the assessment the aunt made it clear this would only be short term until her sister was drug free. The birth father then stated his mother should look after the child. She refused, but the birth father insisted that the social worker must wait until his father arrived from Pakistan, as he was "more reasonable". A local councillor became involved, wanting the maternal grandmother to care for the child, but the assessment found that her poor health made her an unsuitable carer. The birth father's second wife then asked to be assessed. In November 2003, the birth father and his new wife had a baby and thereafter there was no further contact. In 2004 he and his new wife and parents all withdrew their applications and returned to Pakistan.

In total, 81 extended family members were assessed for 61 children. Most (66%) of the assessments found that kin were not able to care for the child: 11 children's relatives withdrew of their own accord, one birth parent objected, one child objected, and in the remaining cases, social workers thought the family was unsuitable.

Twenty-one children (14 of minority ethnicity and seven white children) were placed with kin: about 20 per cent of all the children in the sample. Five of the kin placements broke down very quickly, including two that disrupted because the kinship carer retired and returned to their country of birth, leaving the child behind. The other kinship care disruptions were due to the impact of parental behaviours (one child), abuse of the child (one child) and abuse of the mother as described in the following extract about the kinship placement of a black African child:

Child was placed with maternal aunt and uncle who changed the baby's name without birth parent's consent and blackmailed the birth mother [threatening adoption] to make sure she lived with them as their servant . . .

By the time we concluded our data collection in August 2005 (two to three years after the children became looked after), 16 kinship placements were still intact: 12 for minority ethnic children and four for white children. Most of these placements seemed to be stable and offering good quality care.

Illustrative example

Jayden, child of white/Jamaican/Asian parentage was referred because of neglect and domestic violence. His mother was addicted to heroin and the father was known to the police for supplying drugs, GBH, and gun ownership. Jayden remained with his mother until her early death, due to an overdose. He was placed with a younger sibling in a long-term kinship placement with his maternal aunt and uncle. A Care Order was made because of the father's threats and aggressive behaviours. All reports were of a happy and settled placement, with the aunt and uncle sensitive to the needs of the children.

Matching in foster placements

Ninety-one children had a placement with a foster carer.[11] The foster carer's ethnicity was not routinely recorded on children's files; the "match" had to be ascertained from review forms and other documents found in the file. Even so, we were unable to ascertain the match for 22 per cent of the children in foster care.

Table 5.1 below outlines how well the foster carer(s) and children were matched by ethnicity by the number of foster placements the child

---

[11] Ten children never had a foster placement as they were placed directly with kin, and one child stayed at home on a Care Order.

experienced. In the table, we have chosen to describe any child placed with carers where one carer matched part of their ethnicity as a "partial match". This included mixed ethnicity children placed with white English foster carers. This approach was taken throughout the study. Black children were rarely matched by ethnicity. A few white children were not in ethnically matched placements: some were placed with Asian foster carers and others had white parents who were born in countries outside the UK and ethnically matched foster carers were not available.

Table 5.1
The number of children (n = 91) in ethnically matched foster care placements

Foster Placements	No information available	Not matched	Partial match	Good match
First placement **n = 91**	20	14 7 Mixed 2 White 2 Asian 3 Black	27 18 Mixed 6 White 3 Asian	30 1 Mixed 25 White 4 Asian
Second placement **n = 36**	3	3 1 Mixed 2 White	11 6 Mixed 2 White 3 Asian	19 15 White 3 Asian 1 Black
Third placement **n = 8**		2 1 White 1 Black	3 3 Mixed	3 2 White 1 Asian
Fourth placement **n = 3**			1 1 Mixed	2 2 White
Fifth placement **n = 2**				2 2 White
Sixth placement **n = 2**				2 2 White

Moves and disruptions while the children were looked after

The overall stability of placements was good. Nineteen per cent of children had planned moves but there were also disruptions (unplanned moves) for 18 per cent.

Children (n = 18) with a disrupted placement

Seven children of minority ethnicity and 11 white children experienced one disrupted foster placement. Half of these fostering disruptions were caused by the "retirement" of the carers. The term "retirement" was used on children's files when foster carers chose to no longer work for the authority. However, there was no information about the events that had led up to the retirement or the motivation of the carer. We were particularly concerned to read about infants who were placed direct from hospital with foster carers who "retired" several months later, resulting in a change of placement. It was unclear whether the event had been predictable or not. The second most frequent cause of disruptions was the child's difficult behaviour (five children) followed by suspected abuse by the carer (two children), and two disruptions occurred because the carers were unable to meet the needs of disabled children.

Four children had multiple disruptions and all were the consequence of the carers feeling unable to manage the children's difficult behaviour. In other studies, boys usually experience more disruptions, but in this study, it occurred in the case of 12 girls and six boys. Six of these children were under the age of one, nine were aged between one and five years old and three between six and eight.

Table 5.2 shows the number and type of placements the children had while they were looked after. All the children placed in residential care had had at least two previous failed foster and/or kin placements. All the white children but only 87 per cent of the children of mixed ethnicity were initially placed with a local authority foster carer. More black and Asian children than white or mixed ethnicity children were placed with kin. However, slightly more black and Asian children had more changes of placement.

Table 5.2
Type, number and percentage of placements while children were looked after

Child's ethnicity	LA foster care			IFP carer		Kin carer	Residential	Total number of placements
	1st	2nd	3rd	1st	2nd	1st		
White[12] (n = 46)	46	12	0	4	4	7	4	77
%	100%	25%		8%	8%	15%	8%	
Mixed (n = 31)	27	6	2	6	1	8	3	53
%	87%	19%	6%	3%	3%	26%	10%	
Black/Asian (n = 18) %	18	6	1	1		9		35
	94%	26%	4%			41%		
Total number of placements	**91**	**24**	**3**	**11**	**5**	**24**	**7**	**165**

[12] One child remained home on a care order and therefore did not need a placement.

Sibling placements

There were ten sibling groups (five of minority ethnicity and five white) in the sample. When they first became looked after, three minority ethnic sibling groups and one white group were placed as a sibling group in foster care. The other sibling groups were split. Two sibling groups were later reunited in foster care and one group initially placed together was split because of conflict between the children.

Matching

Although there were statements in case files about the importance of culture and ethnicity, the culture of children was rarely clearly identified. Each broad ethnic category was treated as though it was a homogenous group with a common cultural history and experience and that children's lived experience of this met these preconceptions. In the next file extract, a Bangladeshi child was placed with an Asian family. The family shared the child's Muslim faith but not language:

> [Child's] cultural needs are adequately met by being placed with Asian Muslim family . . . Carer does not speak Sylheti or Bengali. However, [child] has the opportunity to speak to her siblings if she wishes to . . .

Children with Pakistani or Bangladeshi parents were described as Asian and were sometimes placed with carers whose own Asian heritage was very different. However, because the match was "Asian child with Asian carer", the placement was recorded as a "same-race" placement. There were many examples of "same-race" matching based on ethnic categories rather than on the child's individual needs.

Matching mixed ethnicity children

Social workers were concerned and sometimes confused about how to ethnically match mixed ethnicity children. Most described the children in recording as "Black", and deemed their culture to be that of their minority heritage, i.e. that of their father's ethnicity. Therefore, placements with white English foster carers were usually recorded as being "transracial".

We have already noted in Chapter 3 that mixed ethnicity children in this sample had mainly white mothers and usually absent fathers but it was rare to see acknowledgement that the child had other heritages too. The social worker's recording below, describing the foster carer's ability to consider the child's different heritages, was an exception:

> *Recognising that these children are of mixed heritage . . . therefore making sure they have a balance and a clear insight as to all the areas. The carers' own children are also of mixed heritage and therefore they have positive experience of dealing with this . . .*

Placement of infants in foster care

There were very few concerns recorded on children's files about the placement of infant minority ethnic children with white foster carers. The following extract from recording is illustrative of many social workers' thinking about this issue:

> *[Child] is a young baby two-and-a-half months old. His foster carers are white UK and not the same race and culture as [child]. This does not pose a problem for [child] at the age he is now.*

Concerns about the placement only began to be recorded if the carers later applied to become long-term foster carers, adopt the child or, as in the following example, if the child remained with the foster carers for many years:

> *J is a child of shared heritage, white/Asian. He has been brought up within the Catholic faith and identifies himself as Catholic. His language is English. There is concern that J and his brother do not appear to identify with their Asian heritage and consider themselves as white.*

Contact plans

When the children first became looked after, most (90%) had contact planned with at least one parent. For 50 children (32% minority ethnic and 48% white children), contact was planned with both parents. There were no significant differences in the type or frequency of contact by ethnicity.

Surprisingly, perhaps, nearly half of all the children had a plan for contact with their birth fathers. Where no contact was planned (10%), this was because the parents' whereabouts were unknown or they had died.

Table 5.3
Parental contact plans when the children first became looked after

Planned contact	Supervised face-to-face % (n)	Unsupervised face-to-face % (n)	Letters % (n)	Total % (n)
Mother	85 (68)	14 (11)	1 (1)	87 (80)
Father	89 (41)	11 (5)		50 (46)

Face-to-face contact was supervised for the majority and planned to occur at least weekly. Children also had regular planned contact with siblings (28%), with grandparents (24%), with other significant adults (9%) and with step-parents (6%). In a third of the cases, birth parents and/or kin received substantial amounts of practical and emotional support to enable contact to happen; in a further third, support was limited to payment of bus fares or the provision of travel warrants, and in the remaining third, there was no evidence on files of any support being given. Again, there were no statistically significant differences on the likelihood of being offered support because of their ethnicity.

Children's developmental needs while looked after

While the children were looked after, it was recognised that seven per cent had physical disabilities (four minority ethnic and three white children). A greater number (26%) had health conditions (15 minority ethnic and 12 white children) and 13 per cent had learning difficulties (six minority ethnic and seven white children). Although most of the children (74%) were under school age, nearly half of those attending school were in the process of being made subject of a statement of special educational needs (two children of minority ethnicity and ten white children).

There were concerns recorded on files about the emotional and behavioural development of 18 per cent of the children (nine children of minority ethnicity and nine white children). Concerns included sexualised behaviour, unusual play patterns, over-activity and physical harming of others. None of these children had a diagnosed condition. Relationships were also of concern. Difficulty in the child's attachment behaviours were described in 26 per cent of cases (21 minority ethnic and six white children) and difficulty in making and keeping friends in 18 per cent (11 minority ethnic and seven white children).

Identity and self-esteem were rarely mentioned, except in the broadest manner. The researchers looked for any recording of how carers might give the child opportunities to develop and to celebrate cultural traditions, language and religion. This was usually absent and occurred so infrequently that it was not possible to analyse the data.

In 66 per cent of files, there was no mention of whether the child attended a place of worship. In the 10 cases (eight children of minority ethnicity and two white children) where there was some record, parents or relatives took the child in seven cases and in only three cases did the foster carer take the child.

Services while looked after

Twenty-seven per cent of the children received at least one additional service intended to address their needs. These services included attending family centres (12%), and receiving speech therapy (8%), additional support at school (6%), outpatient services (3%) or individual therapy (3%). There were no differences by ethnicity in the proportions receiving additional services.

Permanency planning

For about half the children, the plan was to return home and to do so within six months. Social work plans showed that a third of the children had adoption as the first social work plan. The child's ethnicity did not make a statistical difference to whether adoption or reunification was the type of plan made.

Table 5.4
The social worker's initial plan for the child

The plan for the child	Minority ethnicity children (n = 54) %	White children (n = 48) %
Return home within six months	35 (19)	38 (18)
Adoption	30 (16)	38 (18)
Eventual return home	11 (6)	14 (7)
Long-term placement with relatives/friends	13 (7)	4 (2)
Long-term permanent placement with foster carers	9 (5)	4 (2)
Residential placement	2 (1)	2 (1)

We have already commented on the number of children without a thorough assessment, but there were also many documents missing from files that would have been useful in helping social workers to plan and provide support. There were no health plans for 43 per cent of the children, no personal education plans for 40 per cent of those over four years old, and chronologies were missing in 37 per cent of files. There were more missing documents for minority ethnic children than white children but differences did not quite reach statistical significance. Eight children had none of these documents on file (seven minority ethnic and one white child), and in all but one of these cases the plan was for reunification. There seemed to be less assessment activity when reunification was the plan.

Delay
There was evidence of attempts to reduce delay in planning for the majority (67%) of children. A few (8) cases were subject to concurrent planning, 39 cases involved twin-track planning, and in other files there was evidence of internal mechanisms such as file audits and senior management tracking of looked after children to reduce delay. However,

in 17 per cent of cases, care planning was being developed sequentially, i.e. trying one plan and, if that failed, moving on to the next option.

There were delays for over a third of the children (20% minority ethnic and 15% white children). Most of the delays were due to lengthy legal proceedings, assessments of kin, and parental behaviours, such as going missing or strongly opposing social work plans. The two extracts below, from CAFCASS reports, illustrate the ways in which delays occurred, the dilemmas social workers faced when trying to work in partnership with parents and ensure that every effort had been made to find a family member to care for the child, while at the same time not incurring delay:

> *It is clear now the [local authority] allowed the situation to go for much longer than it should. It seems that over the years perhaps some allowance was made for the historically chaotic nature of the family, the past losses and emotional needs of mother, her pleasant manner, and partial co-operation with services, and the various unplanned crises that occurred. However, key decisions and processes might have been applied earlier, which could have improved the situation for the children . . . Finally, matters were brought to a head by another unplanned crisis when [child] was taken to hospital.*

> *Child is now two-and-a-half years old. It would appear that many months have been lost while the LA were "waiting" to see if the maternal grandmother would present herself as a long-term carer. I therefore feel the LA should have made more vigorous attempts to secure the child's long-term future placement.*

Changes to the permanency plan

The initial placement plan did not change for half the children. Reunification plans changed the most frequently. This had been the initial plan for 50 children but within a year only 11 children had reunification as the aim. Instead, for most, the preferred placement became adoption. There was movement in other plans too (see Figure 5.2). Plans changed because new information became available or assessments revealed additional concerns about children's safety. The actions of birth parents were also very influential, especially when they failed to attend contact visits or planning and review meetings, or showed no interest in their

Figure 5.2
Change in the initial plan

Ethnicity	Initial plan made for children		Second plan
White	Return home (25)	⇨	Adoption (15) Return home (5) Long-term fostering (4) Kinship care (1)
	Adoption (18)		Adoption (17) Kinship care (1)
	Kinship care (5)		Adoption (3) Kinship care (2)
	Long-term fostering (2)		Residential care (1) Long-term fostering (1)
	Residential (1)		Adoption (1)
Black	Return home (4)		No changes in any plans
	Adoption (2)		
	Kinship care (1)		
Asian	Return home (8)	⇨	Adoption (5) Kinship care (3)
	Adoption (3)		Adoption (3)
	Kinship care (3)		Adoption (1) Return home (1) Kinship care (1)
	Long-term fostering (2)		Long-term fostering (1) Adoption (1)
Mixed	Return home (13)	⇨	Adoption (9) Return home (3) Kinship care (1)
	Adoption (11)		Adoption (10) Kinship care (1)
	Kinship care (4)		No changes in kinship care plans
	Long-term fostering (2)		Adoption (1) Long-term fostering (1)
	Residential care (1)		Kinship care (1)

child. Circumstances and families' lives often changed rapidly and not all these plans came to fruition, as we describe in Chapters 6 and 7.

By the end of the data collection in 2005, 16 per cent of children had returned home, 15 per cent were placed with relatives and 17 per cent were looked after with the intention of remaining in care. By far the greatest number (67 per cent) had had an adoption recommendation at some point in their care pathway, and this may be because the sample contained so many very young children. The following chapters examine how the plans made came to fruition.

Summary

- The 102 children were, on average, two years old when first looked after.
- Social workers often made determined efforts to find kin carers and assessed 81 relatives. The majority of kin were unable or unwilling to care for the child and sequential assessments created delay.
- Mixed ethnicity children placed with white foster carers were recorded as being in "transracial" placements and described as "Black". Despite statements about the importance of culture and ethnicity, the culture of children was not clearly identified.
- Very few concerns were recorded about the placing of *young* minority ethnic children with white foster carers, until the carers expressed an interest in becoming the child's long-term foster carer or adopter.
- The ethnicity of the foster carer was not routinely recorded. The majority of children were in a foster care placement that was a good or partial match with their ethnicity.
- Nineteen per cent of children had planned moves and 18 per cent experienced disrupted placements.
- For about half of the children the initial plan was for a quick return home. Few of these plans came to fruition and a year later reunification was the plan for only 11 children. Adoption was the plan for 68 children.
- Many documents needed for matching and planning support were missing from the files.
- There were attempts to reduce delay in 67 per cent of cases, but a third

of the children had no permanency plan in place by four months or their plan was not being acted upon. Most delays were due to legal proceedings, parental behaviours or the assessments of kin.

- Hardly any data were recorded on how carers might give the child opportunities to develop and celebrate their own cultural traditions, language and religion. Identity and self-esteem were rarely mentioned, except in broad terms.
- At the end of data collection, 16 per cent of the children had been reunified, 15 per cent were living with kin and 67 per cent of the children had an adoption recommendation. One child had remained at home throughout.

6 Children with adoption recommendations

This chapter examines the pathways of the 68 children (32 children of minority ethnicity and 36 white children) who had a "should be placed for adoption recommendation" made by a panel. More white children (75% of all the white children) than minority ethnic children (59% of all the minority ethnic children) had an adoption recommendation, but the difference between the groups was not quite statistically significant. The children were on average nearly three years old (range under one year to seven years old), with 53 per cent aged one or under at the time the panel met to consider the recommendation. Again, it is worth noting that black children were older at referral (see Figure 6.1) and therefore older at the time the panel made the recommendation.

Figure 6.1
The children's ages in years at the time of the recommendation

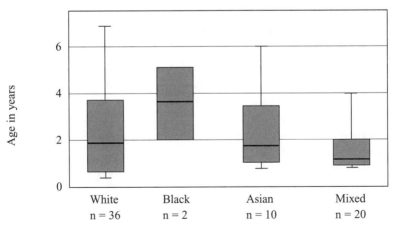

Planning for placement

The three local authorities used BAAF's Form E (now replaced by the Child's Permanence Report) to collect information about the children, but the form was missing from 10 per cent of children's files. Researchers rated the form on a four-point scale with one being poor (these forms had large chunks of information missing and only descriptive writing) and a score of four being given to reports that included good information and analyses. These ratings were not checked between researchers because of time constraints. Researchers rated the majority of the Form Es as being satisfactory with 10 per cent of very high quality.

These assessments gave a thorough account of the child's history, the impact on the child, and considered the kind of family that would be required to meet the child's needs. A few (17%) assessments were poor with gaps in chronologies or sections incomplete. The four-point scale was reduced to a binary score (good/poor) for purposes of analysis. More minority ethnicity children than white children had very poor-quality or missing social work assessments, but the differences did not quite reach statistical significance.

However, there were statistical differences in the quality and type of children's pre-adoption medical reports. In 37 per cent of cases, the only medical reports submitted to panel were the looked after children's annual health assessment. Just fewer than three-quarters of these were on minority ethnicity children.[13] Unlike the BAAF medical forms, these provided only basic information on the health of the child and did not include information on the obstetric history of the mother, the neonatal history of the child, other information on the general health of the birth family or any analysis of future likely areas of concern. The over-emphasis on the "annual medical" or physical examination has been reported in other studies (Department of Health, 2002) and is of particular concern when children are being placed for adoption.

Overall, minority ethnicity children were more likely than white

---

[13] Chi-square = 6.959, (df = 1), p<.008

children to have a poor-quality completed Form E and to have a limited health assessment on their files.

Social workers' placement priorities

The Form E required social workers to tick the categories to be considered when finding and matching adoptive families. Table 6.1 below outlines the main needs of the children identified on the form.

Table 6.1
Matching considerations as identified on the Form E[14] (n = 61) of the children with adoption recommendations

Matching consideration	Minority ethnicity children	White children
	n = 28	n = 33
	%	%
"Same race" placement required	64	24
Emotional and behavioural difficulty	11	36
Sibling group placement required	11	30
Genetic/unknown risks	27	12
Ongoing health condition	14	9
Sexualised behaviour		12
Learning disability		9
Physical disability	4	3

After reading the whole Form E, researchers rated the matching criteria which had been given the most weight and prominence. Over a third of white children had emotional and behavioural difficulties identified or required a sibling placement. "Same-race" placement was the dominant criterion for the majority of minority ethnicity children but this was often described in a brief sentence, as in the example below, and there was little analysis of the child's culture:

---

[14] Seven Form Es were missing from case files

[Child] needs a racially and culturally appropriate placement to help him develop his cultural needs, his language skills and knowledge of his culture.

Where a "same-race" placement was not the dominant consideration for minority ethnicity children, it was usually because one sibling was white and another was of mixed ethnicity and a sibling placement was preferred. However, social workers also tried to balance the wish for a "same-race" placement, a preferred sibling placement and birth parents' wishes, as in the example below:

Illustrative example

Lily was born to a white mother and a mixed ethnicity (white/Asian) father. When Lily became looked after, she was placed with an Asian foster carer. A white family, who had already adopted Lily's siblings, expressed a strong interest in adopting Lily too. The social worker had initial telephone conversations with the adopters and recorded that she had prepared them for some of the issues that would be relevant to their proposal to adopt, the most important being the child's Asian/white heritage. The social worker thought that the key issue with regard to the potential adoptive placement was weighing up the relative merits of a placement with a half-sibling as opposed to finding a family that closely reflected the child's racial heritage. The social worker's notes stated:

Whilst the assessment of this family is ongoing, the adoption unit will also be looking for alternative placements for Lily, specifically placements that reflect her racial origin. Birth father suggested a friend would be a suitable carer for Lily. This friend has converted to the Muslim faith, and he feels she would be able to meet all Lily's ethnic and cultural needs.

Occasionally, the child's ethnicity was unknown and social workers guessed what it might be, using skin colour and other physical characteristics, as in the example below:

He has blond hair and blue eyes. Areas of darker skin pigmentation mean that there is a possibility that he may have a parent or grandparent who is African-Caribbean or Asian. (Social worker's notes)

There were no examples of DNA testing being used to determine children's ethnicity: it was only used to determine paternity.

Many of the children were very young and therefore making confident predictions about their future health and development was not possible. There was uncertainty about the future development of 39 per cent of the children because of their health (e.g. cerebral palsy), incomplete information on the birth parent's health, or uncertainty over the impact of being exposed in the womb to opiates or alcohol, as in the extract below:

When born, [child] was diagnosed with a small ventricular septal defect (hole between the left and right ventricle of the heart). She also has mild dysmorphic features and no philtrum (crease between nose and top lip) as well as thin upper lip – possibly caused by foetal alcohol syndrome . . .

The adopter's Form F

The Form F (now the Prospective Adopter's Report) contains the assessment of the adopters, outlines the kinds of children they feel able to parent, and evaluates the family's strengths and weaknesses. One section of the form asks potential adopters to describe how they value diversity. This is a difficult question to evidence and adopters of white ethnicity gave examples of relatives who were of minority ethnicity or stressed their own personal values or emphasised the diversity of neighbourhoods in which they lived, particularly those from London, as in the extracts from Form Fs below:

We would hope to enable children to learn that all people are of equal worth and that they would learn this through first-hand experience, through mixing with a diverse range of people. I would also aim to be a good role model.

I think one of the good things about living in London is that there are many different cultures and communities here.

Gay and lesbian prospective adopters drew on their own experience of discrimination and thought this would give them additional skills to help children deal with racism, as in the following examples:

We enjoy living in a rich and varied world. Some of our best friends are heterosexual and we have no problem with this. As gay men we feel an affinity with the challenges minority groups face. (Form F section written by the adopters)

Because of their own experiences as gay men of living in society, the adopters have a strong ability to empathise with issues of discrimination and to be aware of how prejudice can impact on people's lives. (Social worker's report)

Some social workers wrote comments on adopters' Form Fs that implied that white adopters were not expected to parent a child with a different ethnicity:

Adoptive parents would love to nurture a child whose ethnicity is different from their own, without question. However, they recognise that they are not in a position to meet the needs of a child from a different culture or ethnicity.

Perhaps as a consequence of not expecting to make "transracial" placements, only the Form Fs of adopters of minority ethnicity had descriptions of how the prospective adopters managed racism in their own and their family's lives, as in the example below:

Both remember days at school when they were called names and discriminated upon on the basis of being Black. They learnt to cope with such attitudes by ignoring negative comments and getting on with whatever they needed to do. The couple have endeavoured to encourage the same approach with their children while instilling in them a sense of self-worth that is regardless of colour.

Contact plans

Contact plans were examined to see what types of contact and frequency were being planned at the time family finding began. Twenty-three of the 68 children had no contact with either parent. Only one child with no parental contact had maintained contact with a relative (a grandparent).

Contact plans had changed for many since they first became looked after. Face-to-face contact was now almost exclusively supervised and was less frequent. Most plans were now for face-to-face contact once or twice a year, although 11 (six minority ethnicity children and five white children) still had bi-monthly supervised face-to-face contact with a parent. In most cases where face-to-face contact had previously been erratic or had stopped, letterbox contact was planned.

Table 6.2
Contact plans for children (n = 68) with an adoption recommendation

Contact planned with	Type of contact	Minority ethnicity (n = 32)		White (n = 36)	
Mothers	Face-to-face	10	31%	8	22%
	Letterbox	7	22%	24	67%
Fathers	Face-to-face	5	16%	4	11%
	Letterbox	3	9%	9	25%
Siblings	Face-to-face	7	22%	7	19%
	Letterbox	0		6	17%
	Phone	1	3%		
Grandparents	Face-to-face	4	12%	4	11%
	Letterbox	2	6%	4	11%
Other	Face-to-face	3	9%	3	8%
	Letterbox			2	5%

Support for contact was provided for 24 children (11 children of minority ethnicity and 13 white children). For the small number of children with paternal contact, it was going well and most of the planned face-to-face contact occurred and was described positively.

For three children (one minority ethnic child and two white children), the quality of the contact visits with birth mothers was of concern, as illustrated in the extract below:

> *Mother's contact has been very sporadic. She never telephones to cancel contact. She just doesn't turn up. During contact she engages in adult conversation or is interrupted by frequent telephone calls from her present partner. Father has been very consistent in his contact with child.*

Family finding

It was hoped that current foster carers or kin would adopt a quarter of the children (no difference by ethnicity) and therefore new adoptive families were sought for three-quarters of them. In the majority (81%) of cases, social workers hoped to find adopters in-house or through local consortium arrangements. However, it was striking how few prospective adoptive families came forward expressing interest in adopting the children.

Family finding for minority ethnicity children (n = 32)

Families were sought for 20 mixed ethnicity, ten Asian and two black children. Only six children were actively promoted through multiple sources, i.e. the consortium, voluntary adoption agencies (VAAs) and family-finding publications such as *Be My Parent* (published by BAAF) and *Children Who Wait* (published by Adoption UK). Information on how social workers tried to find new families was missing from 19 per cent of children's files, and it was not possible to be certain whether any activity had occurred or not. In these cases, it is probably safe to conclude that there was no activity that necessitated financial expenditure.

There was no interest at all shown in two minority ethnicity children. Below is a short extract from the profile of one of these children, a healthy girl of mixed ethnicity (aged two) who was still in foster care at the end of data collection. Writing profiles is an art and the one below limited the possibilities for this little girl:

> *Birth mother is of Ghanaian background (but born in Italy) and a putative father of African-Caribbean background. T is of African-*

Caribbean background. She has black skin, dark brown hair and brown eyes. T needs a family that will reflect her ethnic background and will also reflect her cultural identity.

Only three minority ethnicity children had more than three families come forward expressing interest in adoption, and these children had all been actively promoted through family-finding publications. The majority (67%) of children needing a new family had just one or two interested applicants. Surprisingly, even very young infants (under the age of 12 months) had few adopters expressing interest.

Family finding for white children (n = 36)
A greater number of white children (than minority ethnic children) had had special needs identified such as emotional and behavioural difficulties and so it might be expected that finding adoptive families would be more difficult for them. Seventeen per cent of white children were actively promoted through a variety of means: through the consortium, VAAs, and family-finding publications. Information on recruitment activity was missing from 31 per cent of children's case files, and there appeared to be no activity at all in a further 14 per cent of children's records due to the absence of social workers. White children had more prospective adopters come forward expressing interest (up to 10 prospective families in some cases) and therefore the social worker had more choice. But even so, 38 per cent of white children had only one or two families expressing interest.

Other adults who came forward as potential adopters
While family finding was going on, more foster carers and family members came forward to be considered as suitable adopters. Although there had been a great deal of previous social work assessment activity, the prospect of the child being adopted spurred more family members to come forward or made foster carers realise that the child would be leaving. Extended family members asked to be considered for 15 per cent of the children (five minority ethnic and five white children). Inevitably, new assessments created delay and resulted in no suitable kin adopters for these ten children.

Present foster carers came forward for three white and two minority ethnic children, all of whom were infants and had at least one other "stranger" prospective adopter expressing interest. Social workers strongly opposed three of the five foster carer applications.

Illustrative example

A baby boy, Liam, was born to a young white mother who had received no antenatal care and had abused crack cocaine and alcohol throughout her pregnancy. She refused to disclose who the father was but thought he was a Bangladeshi Muslim. The child went from hospital to live with white English foster carers. Over the next few years, there were six different social workers and staffing gaps and Liam remained with his foster carers. The mother showed no interest in the child, did not visit, was untruthful and changed details of the father's ethnicity several times. After five years, the local authority had an adoption plan and an in-house potential prospective adopter. The prospective adopters were in a mixed relationship but the ethnicity did not completely match that of the child's. The foster carers asked to be considered as adopters but were refused an assessment by the authority and consequently lodged an adoption application with the court to prevent Liam's removal. The local authority accepted that Liam had been well looked after and that he thought of the foster carers as Mum and Dad. The local authority used legislation to support their position in the documents that went before the court:

This is a placement which does not meet her ethnic, cultural needs and dual heritage . . . [The carers] provide a high standard of care for [child]. Mr and Mrs X lodged an application with the court to seek an adoption order in respect of [child]. This is in opposition to the LA's plan to place child with a similar cultural and dual heritage to child. This is in line with the section 22 (5) of the Children Act and standard 2 of the Adoption Standards 2003 which states that children are matched wherever possible with a family that reflects their ethnic origin, cultural background, religion and dual heritage . . .

The court appointed a psychiatrist, who did not support the local authority position, and reported that:

The excellence of the home the [carers] have provided and the care they have given is not in question by any party.

The research evidence on the long-term detrimental effects of "trans-racial" adoption and the detrimental effects of the loss of primary attachment figures were argued in court between the local authority and the psychiatrist. The foster carers' application was eventually successful after a bitter court battle. This case illustrates the possible difficulties which can occur when:

- a child has been with white foster carers for many years before family finding begins;
- mixed ethnicity children are viewed as Black and therefore should not be placed with white adopters;
- research evidence is used to argue both for and against the importance of children's attachments versus identity and cultural needs: some professionals prioritised the importance of a "Black identity" over secure relationships and others vice versa.

A further complication in this case was the lack of clarity about the ethnicity of the birth father. The foster carers did not believe the birth mother's initial accounts of the father's ethnicity partly because the child's physical characteristics appeared white British.

Success in family finding

There was often no recording of the reasons why prospective adopters withdrew. Many seemingly did so of their own accord, but some were not matched because of being unable to meet the emotional and behavioural needs of the child or because they lived too close to the birth family's home. Sixteen per cent of prospective adopters were not considered a match because they were assessed as being unable to meet the child's cultural or religious needs.

At the end of our data collection, there were 52 children living with adopters: 30 white children, of whom 20 had Adoption Orders, and 22 minority ethnicity children, of whom ten had been legally adopted. Most adoptive families had been found "in-house", with ten adoptive placements (19%) found through VAAs and six through other local authorities. Eighteen per cent of minority ethnicity children had been placed outside their local area in comparison with seven per cent of white children. This was often needed to protect the child, as the communities they (and the local authority adopters) came from were small. A careful balancing act was performed to ensure sufficient distance but not too much as to prevent contact from occurring. The kinds of families found are described in Table 6.3 below.

Table 6.3
Types of adoptive families

	Minority ethnicity children (n = 22)	White children (n = 30)
Heterosexual stranger couples	5	18
Single stranger carer	8	2
Gay/lesbian stranger couples	3	7
Foster carers	5	3
Kin carers	1	

Adoptive placements for minority ethnicity children

At the end of our data collection, 22 of the minority ethnic children (two black, three Asian, and 18 mixed ethnicity children – 69% of those with a recommendation for adoption) were living with adoptive families. The majority of children had been placed within 12 months of the adoption recommendation. Five children were subject to delays of 14 to 22 months because of significant health concerns in two cases; in another, a sibling group placement was required; and one child's placement was delayed because the prospective adopters returned to Pakistan without notifying Children's Services.

Ethnicity of adopters for minority ethnicity children (n = 22)

Social workers tried hard to "match" the child's ethnicity category with that of the adopters. However, they were also trying to juggle other factors, for example, the religious and other needs of the child, including wanting to place the child with their siblings as well as pay attention to the wishes of the parents. Workers also recorded concerns about delay and the impact this could have on the child. Thirty-six per cent of minority ethnic children were in what could be described as a "matched" placement, if a match is determined solely on ethnicity.

Sixteen mixed ethnicity children were placed for adoption. Only two were placed with adopters who precisely matched their ethnicity. This is not surprising, as we know that the mixed ethnicity adult population is very small in proportion to the number of children in that population.[15] Four children were placed with adopters who were in mixed relationships, but their ethnicity did not exactly match that of the child's. An example of this is given below where an adoptive family was found for a white/Pakistani child.

Adoptive mother is white British; adoptive father is Indian/Asian from Goa. Although not a match in terms of cultural heritage, the issue of dual heritage is one which they would be equipped to deal with. [. . .] Given the length of time which has passed for J and the lack of permanency for him, given the efforts made to find him an "ideal" match and given the number of prospective adopters who looked at J's situation but did not pursue, it is appropriate to consider a family which could give the security, stability and permanence which he requires, especially if they can meet some of his dual heritage needs. (Social worker's report to the panel)

Ten mixed ethnicity children were placed with adopters who were either single parents or where both partners were of the same ethnicity as each

---

[15] Mixed ethnicity children make up 43–63% of the total "mixed" child and adult population in comparison with white British children who are only 22% of the total white British population. Therefore, there are few adults of mixed ethnicity in the population who could be potential adopters.

other: six with white adopters and four with minority ethnic adopters. The complexity of children's heritages made finding an exact match almost impossible, as in the example below.

> *[The child's] mother is white and her father is Maltese and her maternal grandfather is Anglo/Indian/Asian. It is unlikely that a "perfect match" or one closely resembling it would be able to be obtained within an acceptable timescale; whilst Mr and Mrs X is not a perfect match, they are an acceptable second choice. They live in a culturally diverse area and have an open approach towards acknowledging both birth history and heritage. They intend to actively promote her cultural identity with the use of books, teaching resources and discussion.* (Social worker's report to the panel)

Adoptive placements for white children

More white children (83% of those with an adoption recommendation) had been found adoptive families. Three of these adoptive placements had disrupted: two siblings were physically abused by adopters and removed within six months, and another child's prospective adopters withdrew during introductions. All the children had been placed with stranger adopters. Five white children (14%) were subject to delay before being placed: there were legal delays for three children; a sibling group placement was required for one; and one child had a failed introduction that delayed placement.

Ethnicity of adopters for white children (n=30)

Most (80%) of the white children were placed with adopters who matched their ethnicity. Some (10%) were placed with adopters who were in mixed relationships. Three children were placed with couples where one partner was white British and the other partner was Chinese, or white American, or Malaysian. It was not clear why the scarce resource of mixed ethnicity adopters were matched with a white child. We wondered if this was because the adopters had a pale skin colour and therefore would not have been considered for a child thought of as Black, such as a white/Asian child.

Matching on religion

There was evidence in almost all the children's files that the religious aspects of the match were considered, particularly where the child was Muslim. Six of seven Muslim children went into placements where at least one of the adopters was a Muslim.

Some of the mixed ethnicity children had Christian first names but their religion was recorded as Muslim. This concerned some prospective adopters. In the example below, Asian Muslim adopters were considering adopting a mixed ethnicity white/Asian child:

> *[The adopters] believe that a child's name is very important and if a child placed had an Islamic name they would not want to change that. However, they would like to change the name if it was non-Islamic. They feel that it is important because an English name, for example, would not mean anything to them whereas names are very important within Islam. They feel a child could be stigmatised as a child with a non-Islamic name and would immediately stand out within the family and also within an Islamic school. They are both comfortable with their identity as Asian Muslims and will be able to raise a child to have a positive view of their religion and culture.* (Social worker's report)

Most (80%) of the white children (including those who had no declared religion) were placed in households where the adopters had expressed religious affiliations but were not always practising. The majority of adopters were Church of England, and a few were Roman Catholic, Unitarian, Jewish, Salvationist or Jehovah's Witnesses. The rights of the adopters to practise their religion did not always sit easily with the rights of the child. In the extract below, a white child with no declared religion was placed with adopters who were Jehovah's Witnesses.

> *Because they do not celebrate festivals, children in the wider family get presents at other times of the year. They sometimes have a "presents day" so that the children do not miss out. This is what they intend to do with their own children, so that presents are spread throughout the year and not a lot of things on one festival. They do not celebrate birthdays. They do not agree to blood transfusions on*

religious grounds. However, they think there are viable alternatives . . . (Social worker's report to the panel)

The adoption panel minutes showed that they were concerned about the impact of these beliefs on contact and asked about the letterbox arrangement:

How will adopters cope if birth mother wants to send birthday and Christmas cards?

The social worker responded:

The letterbox arrangement will be made for exchanges at a time of year to avoid this problem. The birth family will be told that cards are not part of the arrangement. (Panel minutes)

Ethnicity used as a category

There was virtually nothing recorded about the culture of White children. There seemed to be an assumption that white British culture was similar regardless of where the child had previously lived. The extracts below are typical of the brief comments on white children's culture:

[Child] is living within a family who reflect the white British culture the same as her own. (Social worker's notes)

And in the following extract, from a case in which a white Irish child was placed with English adopters, the emphasis seemed to be on skin colour rather than ethnicity:

[Child] is in a same-race placement, which is appropriate for his needs. (Social worker's notes)

The emphasis in white children's reports was on white British culture: any cultural differences between the four nations were not examined. Although the word "culture" appeared frequently, it was used to mean a fixed ethnic category and skin colour rather than the child's lived experiences, history, family values and traditions, food, patterns of social interaction and environment, etc. "Asian" was often used as an ethnic category by social workers without distinguishing between the cultures of different Asian communities, as in the extract below:

> ... a child from a Bangladeshi Muslim background who is currently placed within a family from an Indian Muslim background. Culturally, except for language, there is, in my opinion, little difference between them ...

The importance of geography and differences between North and South and the specific cultures attached to areas and regions was only mentioned on one child's file.

As we have seen, minority ethnic children were more frequently placed out of their home area and there was little reflection on the impact this might have on the child.

Sibling adoptive placements

Eighteen children were placed with some or all of their siblings in an adoptive family. There were no differences by ethnicity in the likelihood of being placed with siblings. A third of those placed as a sibling group were placed with gay or lesbian adopters.

Adoption support

Twelve (23%) of the 52 children placed for adoption received additional support: half had speech therapy, four had long-term psychotherapy and four adoptive families received support from a family centre. There were no post-adoption support services recorded for children adopted by foster carers or kin.

Changes of plan

Plans changed for a quarter of the minority ethnicity children and 17 per cent of white children who had had an adoption recommendation. At the end of data collection, three minority ethnic children were placed with kin with adoption no longer being pursued; three minority ethnic children had been returned home; and the remaining children (two minority ethnic children and six white children) were in long-term foster care.

The next chapter considers the pathways of these children who were not placed for adoption and the factors that influenced their placement outcomes.

Summary

- Sixty-eight children had a panel recommendation that they be placed for adoption: 32 minority ethnic and 36 white children.
- Minority ethnic children were more likely than white children to have poor quality Form Es and to have a limited health assessment on their files.
- A greater number of white than minority ethnicity children had emotional and behavioural difficulties identified in their Form E assessments.
- Stranger adopters were sought for three-quarters of the children and the plan was that foster carers or kin would adopt the remaining children.
- Family finding for 19 per cent of minority ethnic children and 17 per cent of white children was pursued through multiple means. The response gave social workers little choice: most minority ethnic children had only one or two possible prospective adopters.
- Although white children attracted a greater response, 38 per cent still had only one or two possible prospective adopters.
- Some relatives and foster carers came forward asking to be considered as suitable adopters. Three of the five foster carer applications were opposed by social workers.
- At the end of data collection, adoptive families had been found for 22 minority ethnic and 30 white children.
- Social workers tried hard to match the child's ethnic category with that of the adopters. However, they were also trying to juggle the religious and other needs of the child and pay attention to the wishes of the parents, without incurring delay. Ethnicity was understood and used almost entirely as a fixed category.
- 80 per cent of white and 36 per cent of minority ethnic children were in a matched placement if the census ethnicity categories are used

as the criteria for a match. This was mainly because the majority of minority ethnic children placed were of mixed ethnicity. Religious matching, particularly for Muslim children, was given a high priority.

- Post-adoption support services were not planned for children adopted by foster carers or kin.
- Plans changed away from adoption placements for a quarter of the minority ethnic children and 17 per cent of white children, who had adoption recommendations.

7   Placement outcomes for children

This chapter examines the pathways of children where there were no current adoption plans and concludes by analysing the factors that influenced all the children's placement outcomes. In 2005, the majority of the minority ethnic children in the sample had placements other than adoption (see Table 7.1).

Table 7.1
Placement outcomes for children at the end of data collection period

Placement outcomes	Child's ethnicity	
	Minority ethnic (n = 54)	White (n = 48)
In an adoptive placement	22 (41%)	30 (63%)
Awaiting an adoptive placement	2 (4%)	–
Reunification with birth parent/s	12 (22%)	4 (8%)
Long-term foster/residential care	7 (13%)	10 (21%)
Long-term kinship care	11 (20%)	4 (8%)

Children who were reunified/living with their birth parent(s) (n = 16)

Fifteen children returned home and one child had always remained at home on a Care Order. Of these, two sibling groups were reunified, so 12 minority ethnic children and four white children returned to nine families. Because of the low numbers reunified and the impact of the sibling groups on analysis, the following simply describes what was known about these families.

None of the children returned home quickly. They had been looked after for between nine months and 3 years 7 months, and most had been looked after for over a year.

These children's case histories were examined to see if there were any

Table 7.2
The gender and ethnicity of children who were reunified/living with birth parents

	Minority ethnicity children	White children	Total
Girls	6	3	9
Boys	6	1	7
Total	**12**	**4**	**16**

differences in the characteristics of those who were reunified and those who continued to be looked after. There were no differences in the extent of reported abuse, the number of parental difficulties or the reason for referral. Children had been returned because composition of the household had changed (usually the violent partner had left) and parental problems had reduced because mothers had received treatment for mental illness or addiction. This is not to suggest that all difficulties had been resolved but that there was enough of a shift for social workers to take a measured risk by returning the children home. A sibling group of three were reunified after a court ordered the return of the children against the advice of the social worker.

Children who were looked after in foster or residential care (n = 17)

Sixteen children (seven minority ethnic and nine white children) were in foster placements and one white girl (who had had multiple disruptions) was in a therapeutic community. The majority (14) of children were placed with a long-term foster carer because it was the best possible placement. Ten of these children had had an earlier adoption recommendation and adoption plans had changed for the following reasons:

- children were settled in a foster placement with siblings and the foster carers wanted to offer permanent care;
- children had frequent contact with their birth mothers and there was still the possibility of reunification;

- one child had refused to leave his foster carer to live with kin;
- one child had no immigration status and it was not known whether the parents were alive or dead;
- one child had serious health problems and the foster carers were fearful that, if they adopted, support would be reduced.

None of these placements had disrupted at the end of data collection. Support in the form of short breaks had been agreed for five of the eight placements and additional CAMHS, educational and health support was in place for half of the children.

Long-term foster care was not the placement of choice for three children who were with foster carers because of a failure to find adoptive families and for one child, for whom there was a breakdown of a kinship adoptive placement. There had been professional disagreement about the decision-making for two of the children. These cases involved dilemmas that were often encountered in the case files.

- Should minority ethnic children be moved from a settled placement just because the foster carer was of white ethnicity?
- Should siblings be split to give the youngest the chance of an adoptive family?

The first issue has already been raised in relation to matching by ethnicity in adoptive placements. However, it was also of concern in foster placements, as in the example below.

Illustrative example

After several previous disruptions, Darren, a mixed ethnicity seven-year-old child was placed with a white English foster carer. The placement had gone very well. Darren had finally found a carer he connected with and contact was regular and positive with his African-Caribbean father. The social worker went to the panel with a plan to approve the placement as long-term fostering. The panel did not support the social worker's plan and the following is an extract from the panel minutes:

The panel did not want to propose long-term fostering and asked if adoption had been looked at . . . The Chair said that the general approach of the panel would not be long-term fostering for a child of seven years and asked that if the current carers were prepared to give a home long term to the child, why not adoption? [. . .] In our view, the identification of a permanent family for [child] should be primarily guided by his needs through adulthood, not by the existence of a placement where he is settled at this moment in time. His emotional responsiveness and the good progress that he has made since becoming looked after are good indicators for the success of an adoptive placement.

However, the guardian and court-appointed psychiatrist disagreed with this view.

It will be very disruptive, even devastating, for [child] to move and he would need to be reassured that by being moved he is not being rejected for trying to belong where he is. It could also have serious impact on his willingness to invest in another family. In particular, I would urge the LA most strongly not to dismiss the offer of what is essentially all they would reasonably want in an adoptive placement simply on the grounds that the current carers are not able to offer it [adoption].

The birth father also wanted his son to stay with the carer. He had a good relationship with the white foster carer and felt welcomed when he arrived for contact.

[Father] does not agree that [the child] should be placed with a black family. He thinks he should be able to provide [the child] with appropriate culture and ethnic experience. He also believes it is significant that [the child's] mother is white and half-siblings. He does not feel it appropriate that social services would consider moving [the child] based on racial issues.

Eventually, after a further year, the long-term foster care placement was confirmed as such. This example is also interesting because it raises issues about whose role it is to educate children about their cultural heritage. Clearly, in this case the father thought it was his. In most children's files we read, Children's Services expected the foster carers or adopters to be the primary and often the only adults involved in helping the child understand their cultural heritage.

The second example involves a sibling group and the professional disagreement about the type of permanent placement that should be sought.

Illustrative example – sibling placements

Becky was a white child, the youngest of four, whose mother was violent and had learning difficulties. All the children were removed from home and placed together in foster care when Becky was under a year old. The plan was for the siblings to be adopted but no adopters could be found to take the sibling group. Each child had special needs including Becky, who had very specific health needs. Becky's social worker wanted her to be separated from her siblings and placed for adoption. The family placement team, on the other hand, wanted to keep the siblings together and eventually the adoption panel rescinded the adoption recommendation and decided that the children should remain with their foster carer.

Long-term placements with relatives (n = 15)

At the end of data collection, 15 children (11 minority ethnic and four white children) were living with relatives. These had become long-term placements and Residence Orders had been made in three cases. The children had been looked after from 5–42 months before being placed with kin. Most kinship placements seemed to be going well and there were few documented concerns. In a few cases, there were concerns about the additional stress placed on relatives, and the shortage of large council houses meant that some families were severely overcrowded, as in the example below.

Illustrative example

Saeed was one of four. His parents had a history of domestic violence, and of separating and then reuniting. Eventually, after evidence of physical and abuse, the children became looked after and an adoption recommendation was made. None of the relatives felt able to care for the children because of their own family circumstances. After a family meeting, an uncle and aunt were nominated by the family and the decision was made to split the children – two living with an uncle and two with the paternal grandfather. The houses were in disrepair, damp and very overcrowded (eight people were living in a two-bedroom home), and although Children's Services and the court recommended re-housing, there was a shortage of four-bedroom homes in the area and no indication of when one might become available. The children seemed well cared for, but the relatives were beginning to comment on the children's behavioural difficulties. The guardian and social worker both noted that the family had not really appreciated the severity of the children's behavioural difficulties.

In comparison with adoptive and foster placements, matching on ethnicity was not a key requirement in kinship placements. There was an assumption that because kin were related they would be able to meet the child's needs. However, three of the 15 children were placed with relatives whom they had never met and where there were no established relationships, as in the following example.

Illustrative example

Although born in the EU, Emmanuel (African/Italian) spent the first five years of his life in England (including three years with a white foster carer). When he was five years old, he was placed in Italy with his grandfather, who had little English, and into a school where no one spoke English and where he was the only minority ethnic child. There was no further contact with social workers in England.

Pathways and outcomes

The previous chapters have described the pathways for a sample of young children who all became looked after during 2002 and 2003. We now examine questions about whether minority ethnic children experienced more delay in decision-making and the factors influencing their pathways. It has been suggested that minority ethnic children are dealt with more harshly and enter care more quickly than white children (Barn, 1993). In this sample, there were no statistical differences between white and minority ethnicity children in the age at referral or in their speed of entry to care. However, there were some interesting patterns in the data. At referral, Asian children were the youngest but also the slowest to become looked after. Black children were referred at older ages and they and the mixed ethnicity children entered care fastest.

Children with adoption recommendations

Previous research (Ivaldi, 2000) found that minority ethnic children waited longer than white children at every stage of the adoption process, and that it took 300 days longer on average for them to be placed for adoption. This study was designed to understand more about what created these delays. Data were collected on the length of time between key decision points: length of time from key referral to becoming looked after, to the date of the adoption panel, to matching, and to placement.

In this present sample, once children became looked after, black and Asian children waited longest for an adoption recommendation and this was statistically significant.[16] However, this finding has to be treated with caution since there were only two black and nine Asian children with adoption recommendations.

There were also statistical differences between white and minority ethnic children with an adoption recommendation in the likelihood of being placed for adoption,[17] with white children being more likely to be placed for adoption. To understand more about the factors influencing the chances of being adopted, a binary logistic regression was conducted

---

[16] Anova F (3, 64) = 2.72, p<.05
[17] Fisher's Exact p = .02

using adopted/not adopted as the dependent variable. Black children were excluded, as only two had had an adoption recommendation. In the first step, age at the time of the adoption recommendation and gender were included, but only age was significant (p< .001). As age increased, so did the odds of not being adopted. In the next step, ethnicity was included and was also significant (p<.027), with Asian children the least likely to be adopted.[18] To examine the impact of age further, the whole sample was divided into four groups based on the child's age when they first became looked after:

a) under one
b) aged 1–3 years
c) aged 3–5 years
d) over 5 years old.

The chances of being adopted diminished rapidly for children three years and older, as can be seen in the table below.

Table 7.3
The percentage of children who were in adoptive placements or still looked after 26–40 months after entry to care (by age group)[19]

	Infants %	*Toddlers %*	*3–5yrs %*	*5yrs + %*
Adoptive placement	69	54	33	6
Looked after	6	5	42	59

The four age groups were also compared with the children's placement outcomes at the end of data collection:

a) reunified (16%)
b) placed with family and friends (15%)
c) adopted (51%)
d) remained in foster care/residential (18%)

---

[18] See Figure 7.1
[19] Reunification and kinship care outcomes excluded from this table

The following pie charts show pictorially how age and ethnicity had an impact on placement. Asian children had a greater likelihood of being reunified than white or mixed ethnicity children,[20] a pattern also found in Owen and Statham's analysis (2009) of national datasets. There were no statistical differences in the likelihood of being placed with kin.

Further analyses examined the influence of matching criteria (from children's Form Es) such as sibling group placement, uncertain or developmental delay, genetic or mental health risks, but none was

Figure 7.1

Age at entry to care, ethnicity and placement outcome

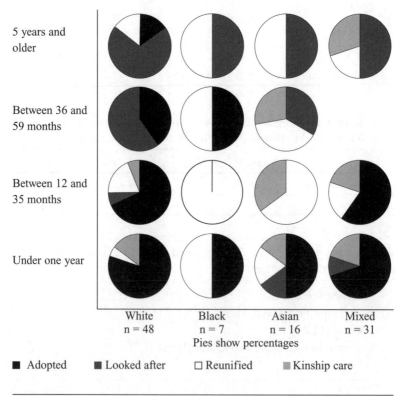

| | White | Black | Asian | Mixed |
| | n = 48 | n = 7 | n = 16 | n = 31 |

Pies show percentages

■ Adopted　　■ Looked after　　□ Reunified　　▨ Kinship care

---

[20]　Fisher's Exact p = .001

significant. Although ethnicity was a significant factor in predicting whether a child would be adopted or not, of much greater importance was the child's age at the time of the adoption recommendation. Of course, it should be noted that this is affected by the speed of social work decision-making and practice within individual local authorities.

The lengthening odds of being adopted at older ages have been noted in previous research (Selwyn et al, 2006) and can also be seen in national data on adoption (DCSF, 2009). However, children's files are not a good source of understanding why these older children were not adopted. We do not know whether social workers had already decided that the children were unadoptable and therefore made less effort, or whether it was a lack of prospective adopters, or other factors. These aspects are examined in Chapters 11 and 12, drawing on the interviews with social workers.

Further analysis using the Kaplan–Meier procedure was undertaken to estimate time to adoptive placement for children within the minority ethnic group. This procedure takes all cases into account, i.e. children with adoption recommendations who were never placed. We decided to combine the Asian and black children for this analysis because of low sample numbers. Time was calculated from the date of the adoption recommendation to the date the child moved into an adoptive placement. Figure A1 in Appendix II illustrates the probability and speed of being placed for adoption from the time of the adoption recommendation for the three groups. Half of the white and mixed ethnicity children were placed by 47 and 41 weeks respectively. In comparison, black and Asian children took longer (59 weeks) to be placed for adoption.

White and mixed ethnicity children continued to be placed for adoption over time until the probability of being adopted levelled off at around a hundred weeks. Black and Asian children's chances of being adopted levelled out far sooner. However, this levelling off should be treated with caution as it is affected by the sample numbers, and the smaller numbers in the black/Asian group may have led to the plot levelling off sooner.

Further analysis of time was conducted using the period between becoming looked after until moving into an adoptive placement or change of plan. During this time period, 50 per cent of mixed ethnicity children had been placed by 19 months, 50 per cent of white children were placed by 23 months and 50 per cent of black and Asian children by 28 months. This confirmed that mixed ethnicity children moved faster through the system and were placed for adoption more speedily than black or Asian children. The pathways of the mixed ethnicity children resembled that of the white children. However, the Kaplan–Meier procedure only allows for the analysis of one factor against "time", and therefore, in the following chapters, other types of regression analysis are used to examine multiple contributing factors.

Overview of the comparative sample

This stratified sample was selected to compare planning, decision-making and outcomes for white and minority ethnic children. There were striking differences in the quality of assessments and consequently the articulation of children's needs in Form Es. We had expected to confirm Ivaldi's work on greater delays for minority ethnic children but found a far more complicated picture. In the present sample, there was evidence that the white and mixed ethnicity groups had similar characteristics and pathways, while Black and Asian children, who made up far smaller proportions of young looked after children, had different pathways.

The recording in children's files showed that great efforts were made to place sibling groups together and to place children in ethnically matched adoptive placements, although there was a tendency to see ethnicity as a fixed category and of primary importance. Numbers in the comparative sample were small, but there were indications that mixed ethnicity children had different histories to those of Asian or black African children. So to provide a check on findings and to understand more about the variations, the second sample (adoption recommended) was used to answer questions about differences within the minority ethnic group and to address the influence of the local authority's policy and practice on outcomes.

Unlike the comparison sample, *all* the children in the *adoption recommended* sample had a panel recommendation that they should be placed for adoption and all were from a minority ethnic group. The following chapters focus on why this group of minority ethnic children became looked after, the stability and match of their placements, and their placement outcomes.

Summary

- At the end of data collection, 51 per cent of the children were in adoptive placements, 16 per cent in long-term foster care, 16 per cent had been reunified, 15 per cent were cared for by extended family and one per cent were in residential care.
- Children who were reunified did not return home quickly: most had been looked after for longer than 12 months.
- Asian children were more likely than white or mixed ethnicity children to be reunified.
- Of the 68 children with adoption recommendations, nearly a quarter (24%) had the recommendation rescinded.
- Professional disagreements often focused on two issues: a) should minority ethnic children be moved from a white foster carer where they were happy and where the carer was offering to become a long-term foster carer?; and b) should siblings be split to give the youngest the chance of an adoptive family?
- There were no statistical differences between white and minority ethnic children in their ages at entry to care or the speed at which they became looked after. But there were differences in the length of time taken to make an adoption recommendation, with Asian and black children waiting the longest.
- The child's age and ethnicity at the time of the adoption recommendation were important factors in whether an adoptive placement was found.

The adoption
recommended sample

8   The adoption recommended sample: from referral to becoming looked after

The sample

The children in the adoption recommended sample included all the children of minority ethnicity with an adoption recommendation (n = 120) made by a panel in our three local authorities between 1 April 2003 and 31 June 2005. The purpose of this part of the study was to have a large enough sample to explore the variation within this group, to examine any differences by local authority, and to test out whether the findings in the comparison sample would remain statistically significant with a larger sample.

Characteristics of the 120 children and their families

The ethnicity of children in the sample reflected the national picture of adopted children, in that mixed ethnicity children (69%) were the largest

Table 8.1
Children's ethnicity as recorded on the children's files

	Ethnicity	*Number*	*Sub group total*
Mixed ethnicity	White/black Caribbean	36	69%
	White/Asian	23	
	Mixed other	20	
	White/Black African	4	
Asian	Pakistani	14	21%
	Bangladeshi	10	
	Asian other	1	
Black	Black African	8	10%
	Black Caribbean	4	
Total		**120**	**100%**

proportion of minority ethnic children with adoption recommendations (see Table 8.1).

The sample was split evenly in relation to gender, containing 60 boys and 60 girls with no significant gender differences between ethnic groups. The majority of children could speak English and 18 per cent were bilingual. Twelve children (10%) were non-English speakers and spoke a variety of languages: Punjabi (5), Sylheti (4), Portuguese (2) and Pashto (1). As the sample included all the minority ethnic children with adoption recommendations, it naturally contained some sibling groups. There were 16 of these: 11 of mixed ethnicity, three Asian and two black sibling groups.

The child's religion was not recorded in 12 per cent of children's files and 30 per cent were described as having no religion. A third of black children and 20 per cent of mixed ethnicity children were Christian, while all the Asian children were Muslim, as were a third of black and 11 per cent of mixed ethnicity children.

Many of the characteristics of the children in this sample were similar to those in the comparison sample. For example, more than half (66%) of them had been referred previously or at the time of their birth. The small group of black children were on average older at the time of referral. The London borough was different from the other two in that black and Asian, but not mixed ethnicity, children were much older at referral (see Table 8.2). This authority had more black African and Asian children who were older when they had arrived in the UK or in the borough.

There were also differences in other characteristics of the children. Mixed ethnicity children had more identified special needs, and three-quarters had a sibling of an ethnicity different to theirs (see Table 8.3).

A significant number of mixed ethnicity children were born testing positive to a range of drugs or showing symptoms of foetal alcohol spectrum disorder (FASD). In some cases, mothers had used a combination of drugs and substances during pregnancy with the impact on the child's development unknown, as in the examples below:

> . . . concerns over mum's abuse of butane gas since she was 12 and throughout her pregnancy. Infant has observations for the unknown effects of butane gas.

Table 8.2
The children's average age in months at referral and by local authority

The child's ethnicity	Number	Local authority	Average age in months at referral
Black	6	Midlands	2
	6	London borough	81
Asian	13	North	3
	2	Midlands	0*
	10	London borough	37
Mixed	27	North	6
	28	Midlands	7
	28	London borough	6

* These cases had been referred before birth.

Table 8.3
Characteristics of minority ethnic children with adoption recommendations

	Black (n = 12) %	Asian (n = 25) %	Mixed (n = 83) %
First-born child of the family	25	36	23
Siblings of different ethnicity	17	0	75*
Nationality other than British	47	4	0**
Physical disability	0	4	7
Health condition	0	12	20
Learning disability	8	0	10
Born with FASD symptoms/ neo-natal abstinence syndrome	8	8	30***

* Fisher's Exact p = .000
** Fisher's Exact p = .000
***Fisher's Exact p = 0.04

Anthony was born positive to cocaine, opiates and diazepam.

Although the number of infants affected by these substances may seem high, children who were referred after infancy had little recorded about their neonatal history and this was particularly the case if children did not have an adoption medical. Therefore, there may have been other children who had been exposed *in utero* to drugs and alcohol but where information was not recorded on the file.

Characteristics of the birth mothers

The differences between the ethnic groups became more apparent when we compared the characteristics of the birth mothers. The characteristics of mothers are reported per family (n = 88), so that mothers of siblings are not double counted. There were too many missing data on children's files to be able to report the characteristics of birth fathers; this was often because the father had been unwilling to give information or was unknown.

There were no significant differences by ethnicity in the mother's age when the study child was first referred to Children's Services, but mixed ethnicity mothers were on average the youngest (23 years) and black mothers the oldest (29 years).

The majority of mothers of these mixed ethnicity children were white or of mixed ethnicity themselves. They had often been in care themselves, had had abusive childhoods, and had become involved in drug/alcohol abuse, often linked to prostitution. They had fragile partnerships with men who were also addicts, usually absent and able to offer little or no parenting support. Many mothers were isolated and had no contact with their own extended families or received no support from them.

There were statistically significant differences in a number of areas (see Table 8.4). Black African and Asian mothers were more likely to have been born outside the UK and to need an interpreter. There were no significant differences, according to the mothers' ethnicity, in the rates of reported learning difficulties, but more mental heath problems were reported among black mothers. It should be remembered that the ethnic category "black" included mothers who were African-Caribbean (6) and black African (8).

Table 8.4
Characteristics of the birth mothers (n = 88) of the minority ethnic children

Ethnicity of mothers	White (n = 39) %	Mixed (n = 18) %	Asian (n = 17) %	Black (n = 14) %	Statistical significance
Born outside the UK	0	0	53	43	p = 0.00
Interpreter needed	0	0	18	28	p = 0.00
In care during childhood	41	78	0	14	p = 0.00
Victim of childhood abuse or neglect	61	83	18	36	p = 0.00
Learning difficulties	20	22	17	14	ns
Mental health problems	31	27	41	50	ns
Involvement in crime	69	72	12	50	p = 0.00
Maternal history of violent behaviour	23	61	6	28	p = 0.00
Served prison sentence	38	39	12	29	ns
Problem drinking	56	61	6	29	p = 0.00
Drug misuse	72	83	12	36	p = 0.00
Domestic violence	64	56	41	36	ns
Other children in care or adopted	52	56	41	43	ns
More than four children	15	28	12	14	ns

There were too few black mothers overall to be able to compare these two sub-groups. However, the African-Caribbean mothers were born in the UK and had similar problems of drug and alcohol misuse as did the white mothers. Black African mothers (8), on the other hand, had come from countries such as Angola, Zimbabwe and Nigeria, and often reported mental health difficulties. There was not enough information on files to know how far mental health problems were connected with experiences in or traumatic dislocations from the country of their birth. These areas were rarely assessed, perhaps because of language difficulties.

Households

Most of the children came from households where the mother was their main carer. Similar to the findings in the comparison sample, fathers were usually absent from the homes of black and mixed ethnicity children, but were present for more Asian children. Five children were living with grandparents and three were privately fostered with family friends at the time of the referral. More Asian children (52%) had siblings and other relatives (20%) sharing their home than did children of other ethnicities. There were just a few mixed ethnicity (6%) and black (8%) children who shared their home with a grandparent or other relative.

Factors leading to the children becoming looked after

There were three main clusters of factors that led to the key referral and ultimately to the children becoming looked after:

* family honour (*izzat*);
* severe maternal mental illness, often combined with domestic violence; and
* parental drug/alcohol misuse.

Family honour

Many Asian children (13) became looked after because of issues of family honour (*izzat*), although to some extent this was also an issue for two black mothers and for two white mothers with Asian partners. Family honour for the white mothers of mixed ethnicity children led to them relinquishing their children on account of shame and racism within their own families on account the birth father was not white. These two white mothers were also very young: under 16 years of age.

In contrast, *izzat* for the Asian mothers was much more of an all-encompassing concept, which would bring disrepute on themselves and their wider family. *Izzat* is an Urdu term referring to the honour or reputation of a person, family or community. It is a concept that has currency in different South Asian contexts. In the context of the family, this means that individuals are expected to put the honour of the family first and to avoid any behaviour that might bring shame on the family. The concept of *izzat* applies to both women and men in the family. However, there is a strong emphasis on the need for teenage girls and women to preserve the honour of the family by observing certain Islamic codes of dress and behaviour, for example, having sex only within marriage; agreeing to an arranged or, in some cases, forced marriage; producing children, especially sons; not going outside the family for help with problems such as domestic violence or child abuse; and not seeking a divorce. However, having mental health problems, being gay or lesbian or failing to do well at school could also be seen as issues of *izzat*. The community can sometimes reject a person who is seen to have brought their family into disrepute.

Six Asian mothers concealed their pregnancies and relinquished their babies because the child had been born either illegitimately, or as the result of rape. They were fearful of the dishonour the child would bring upon their family, of the effects upon future arranged marriages, and of the reactions of their family and their community, as illustrated in the extract below.

> *Birth mother believes she has no option but to have the baby adopted due to her being pregnant outside of marriage and not having the support of the baby's father. She is concerned that the community and her family will isolate her and label her as a bad person . . . Birth mother is concerned that if she keeps the baby her future would be affected in terms of her marriage proposals. Her mother has arranged a marriage and she does not want the marriage to fall through, as it would leave her mother distraught.* (Social worker's recording)

In some cases, women were fearful of violence from brothers, husbands and extended family members. Examples included a mother who was thrown downstairs by a brother in an attempt to terminate her pregnancy, a mother who was locked up in a house, and families who made it impossible for the birth mother to keep the child because of their violent attacks on the birth father.

Mental illness and domestic violence

Domestic violence was prevalent in many families and prevented many mothers from being able to protect their children. However, the mother's neglect of the child was often the focus of social work intervention and there were few mentions of the need to protect and support mothers, as in the example below.

Illustrative example (Asian mother)

The family had been known to Children's Services for many years because of the mother's failure to attend any antenatal or postnatal appointments and because of domestic violence, including a number of severe assaults. No action had been taken due to "lack of evidence". The father later assaulted his previous wife and was imprisoned. During this period he was said to have become a more observant Muslim. This led the social worker to note on his discharge: 'Birth father is now a devout Muslim and his religious beliefs should militate against impulsive anger'. However, the workers became increasingly concerned about the birth mother's whereabouts, as her husband did not allow her to be seen. Eventually, after the father refused medical treatment for one of his children who had meningitis, saying he was going home to pray, police took out a Police Protection Order. They found the home conditions to be extremely poor. All five children and the parents had been sleeping in one double bed and two of the children had meningitis.

Domestic violence was also often recorded in families where mothers had mental health problems. There were high levels of recorded maternal mental illness (see Table 8.4). However, we have already commented on the lack of recording of the onset and possible causes of the illness and social work assessments did not connect mental illness, domestic violence and the inability to protect the child.

Illustrative example (black African mother)

Asad's birth parents were African and arrived in the UK seeking asylum. Asad first came to the attention of Children's Services after the health visitor became concerned about his mother's mental health. Asad became looked after and there were several attempts at reunification but all failed because of the injuries he had sustained and physical aggression from the father.

Alcohol and drug misuse

The great majority of mothers for whom alcohol and drug misuse were of concern were white or of mixed ethnicity, but these concerns were also the main reason why the children of four of the African-Caribbean mothers had been referred. These mothers had often been in care themselves, had had abusive childhoods, and had become involved in drug/alcohol misuse, which was often linked to prostitution and crime. They had fragile partnerships with men who were also addicts, usually absent and able to offer little or no parenting support.

Illustrative example (white mother)
Anita was born to a white mother who had a chaotic lifestyle and was known to misuse drugs and alcohol, self-harm and be involved in prostitution. The mother had had a previous child removed from her care due to neglect and physical abuse. However, because the mother had made great improvements, Anita was placed with her mother from hospital. However, soon afterwards the mother lapsed and returned to her previous lifestyle. She was charged with theft and assault and there were further suicide attempts. The baby quickly became looked after due to concerns of neglect and abuse.

The use of private fostering

There were a few cases where other reasons played a part in the child becoming looked after. One Asian child and two black children had been brought to the UK as infants by their affluent parents and left with friends, perhaps in the belief that the children would have a better life and more opportunities. Once the children were brought to the UK, there was no evidence on children's files that parents had kept in touch. Recording on files suggested that the children had been more fearful of disclosing abuse because of the efforts their parents had made to bring them to the UK. The children became looked after because of severe abuse and neglect by their private foster carer.

Illustrative example (African mother)

Ruth's father, a wealthy businessman, placed his daughter and two cousins with a family friend in England. Children's Services received a referral from Ruth's school, when she was 10 years old, expressing concern that Ruth was being physically abused by the carer and sexually abused by a cousin. The child had been threatened with return to Africa if she disclosed this. The cousin was convicted on three counts of rape and the carer was charged with cruelty and neglect.

Services

There were similar patterns of service use in this sample as in the comparison sample. It was again striking that, although domestic violence was prevalent across all ethnic groups, only three mothers used a refuge (one white, one black African and one Pakistani). Twenty per cent of children received additional services from hospital outpatient clinics, in particular, paediatric services, primarily to help with developmental problems, and just over a third of families attended a family centre.

A large proportion of parents in the adoption recommended sample refused or failed to take up services. In the comparison sample, 16 per cent of parents had refused a service, while in this sample 45 per cent had refused additional social services or health services (18%) or mental health (12%) or education (3%) services. There was no statistical difference between ethnicities or local authorities in terms of the likelihood of taking up services. It was striking that there were so many services offered which parents refused or did not benefit from, for example, by failing to turn up for appointments. One of the reasons that the children went on to have adoption recommendations was parental lack of engagement with professionals and refusal to accept services.

Plans and assessments when first looked after

The plans for the children when they first became looked after, their ethnicity and their local authority are listed in Table 8.5. Significantly, more children from the London borough had reunification plans, while more children from the North had plans for substitute care.[21]

Table 8.5
The plan for the child at entry to care by ethnicity and local authority

The plan at entry to care	Child's ethnicity				Authority	
	Black (n = 12) %	Asian (n = 25) %	Mixed (n = 83) %	North (n = 40) %	Midlands (n = 36) %	London (n = 44) %
Return home	50	48	34	23	39	52
Long-term placement with kin	8	8	7	–	11	11
Long-term placements with foster carers	17	4	–	2	–	5
Adoption	25	40	57	70	50	32
Twin-track planning	–	–	2	5	–	–

Kin assessments

Over three-quarters of the children (78%) had relatives assessed for their suitability to provide care for them, a similar proportion to that found in the comparison sample. The London borough conducted significantly more kin assessments (75%) than the other two authorities[22] (North 50%, Midlands 69%). This may be because the borough had a dedicated kinship care team. Just as in the comparison sample, children often had relatives coming forward sequentially, which led to multiple assessments that resulted in delayed court proceedings and decision-making. Only 11 (9%) children were eventually placed with relatives, as assessed relatives were often deemed unsuitable or withdrew of their own accord (30%). There were no differences between the ethnicities or authorities on the number

---

[21] Fisher's Exact p = .010
[22] Fisher's Exact p = .049

of relatives coming forward, or the reasons why children were not placed with kin.

Placements

During the time the children were looked after (before an adoption recommendation had been made), 12 per cent of children had failed attempts at reunification.

Sibling placements

The sample contained 16 sibling groups amounting to 48 children. Social workers tried to keep sibling groups together. Only three of the children were separated from a brother or sister in foster care: two children were in separate foster homes because of the severity of their special needs but were later adopted together and the other child (white/Asian) was separated from her sibling (white/Caribbean) because the social worker thought this was necessary to comply with the local authority's "same-race" policy.[23]

Disrupted placements

A quarter of the children had disrupted placements (five black, seven Asian and 19 children of mixed ethnicity). Most of the disruptions were in foster care but a third were kinship care disruptions. A small number of mixed ethnicity children (4) had multiple disruptions (>3) caused by their challenging behaviour. The reasons for disruption followed the same pattern as in the comparison sample. The carer's "retirement" was the most frequent reason why the placement ended.

Ethnicity of the carers while children were being looked after

Most children had two placements on average (range 1–6). The percentage of carers matched with the children's ethnicities at each placement is shown in Figure 8.1. In the figure, we have chosen to describe placements where one part of a child's ethnicity is matched – often a mixed ethnicity child with a white carer – as a partial match.

---

[23] Senior managers within the local authority stated that no such policy existed.

Figure 8.1
The average percentage of carers matched by the child's ethnic group

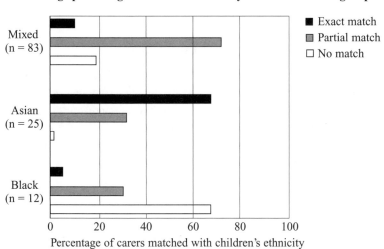

Percentage of carers matched with children's ethnicity

Most Asian children (67%) were in placements where their ethnicity was matched exactly with that of their carer, and most mixed ethnicity children (71%) had a carer who matched a part of their ethnicity. In contrast, there was no match for the majority (66%) of the black children. Social workers sometimes moved children in a planned way to a foster placement which would better meet their cultural and language needs, but occasionally the wish for a "same-race" placement was applied without considering other aspects of a child's needs, such as their emotional needs and attachments, as in the following example.

Illustrative example

Sakina and Razia, two Bangladeshi Muslim children, were placed with a Pakistani Muslim foster family. It was recognised, at the time of the placement, that there were language differences but the girls remained there for two years and they expected and wanted to stay. During this time no concerns were raised, the girls were developing well, and no additional support had been offered. However, the social worker decided that the girls should be moved (against the children's wishes) to another placement because of a "same-race" policy.

Making the adoption recommendation

This sample was selected because all the children had a panel recommendation that they be placed for adoption. The children were looked after for an average of ten months before that recommendation was made (range 0–54 months, s.d 8.7). The next chapter follows the children from the time of the adoption recommendation to the time data collection ceased in January 2007.

Summary

- The sample comprised all the minority ethnic children (n = 120) with an adoption recommendation made between 2003 and 2005 in the three local authorities.
- The children's characteristics were similar to those of minority ethnic children in the comparison sample. Mixed ethnicity children had more special needs identified and three-quarters had a sibling of an ethnicity different to theirs.
- The majority of birth mothers were white or of mixed ethnicity. Their characteristics and histories were different from those of Asian or black mothers. Many parents refused services and were not engaged with service providers.
- There were three main clusters of factors that had led to the children becoming looked after. These were family honour (*izzat*), severe maternal mental illness, and drug and alcohol abuse. More Asian children were relinquished and became looked after because of issues of family honour.
- Local authorities were aware of the importance of trying to keep siblings together: 88 per cent of the children were placed in foster care with all or some of their siblings or were reunited with siblings later.
- Over three-quarters of the children had relatives assessed for their suitability to care for the children. Assessments were often undertaken sequentially and this contributed to delay.

- The London borough conducted more kin assessments and had reunification as the plan for more children than the other two local authorities,
- Most Asian children (67%) were in placements where their ethnicity was matched exactly with that of their carer, and most mixed ethnicity children (71%) had a carer who matched one part of their ethnicity. In contrast, there was no match for the majority (66%) of the black children.

9   Adoption planning and placement outcomes

Many (50%) of the children were less than 15 months of age when their cases went to the adoption panel. At the time the panel made an adoption recommendation, the black and Asian children from the London borough were older when compared with the mixed ethnicity children in that borough[24] and with the black[25] and the Asian[26] children in the other two authorities. This was partly explained by black and Asian children being older at referral in the London borough but this did not explain why Asian children had waited longer before the recommendation had been made (see Table 9.1).

We knew the London borough had a kinship care team and had conducted more kinship assessments than the other two local authorities, so we examined whether these assessments were delaying the decision. All the Asian children in the London borough had kin assessed as possible carers, but so had 79 per cent of the children of mixed ethnicity and they had not been subject to delay. However, we had not collected data on the number of kin who had been assessed and lived outside the UK. Therefore we do not know if overseas assessments were a factor in Asian children waiting longer for an adoption recommendation.

Family finding

Many of the children would be thought of as "hard to place" because of their ethnicity, age, and special needs. We had assumed that the older children would have been the ones chosen for promotion in family-finding efforts but more (59%) mixed ethnicity children (the youngest group) were promoted in family-finding publications than Asian (37%) or

---

[24]   Kruskal-Wallis test, $p<.00$

[25]   Kruskal-Wallis test, $p<.05$

[26]   Kruskal-Wallis test, $p<.01$

Table 9.1
Children's average age in months at referral, when looked after and at the time of the adoption recommendation

Child's ethnicity	Number of children	Local authority	Age at referral	Age when looked after	Age at adoption recommendation	Months between becoming looked after and adoption recommendation
Black	6	Midlands	2	4	18	15
	6	London borough	81	97	110	13
Asian	13	North	3	12	18	6
	2	Midlands	0	3	12	9
	10	London borough	37	65	87	22
Mixed	27	North	6	14	21	7
	28	Midlands	7	25	34	9
	28	London borough	6	17	26	10

black (27%) children. Surprisingly, the gender and the child's age at panel were not associated with whether or not the child was promoted. The London borough used promotion more than the other two local authorities did and this difference was statistically significant (p = .004).

Table 9.2
Promotion of children through family-finding publications in the three authorities (n = 95)[27]

Child's ethnicity		North (n = 32)	Midlands (n = 24)	London (n = 39)
Not promoted		18 (56%)	15 (63%)	10 (26%)
Promoted	Black	–	3	0
	Asian	1	1	5
	Mixed	13	5	24

Matching considerations

We found the same weight given to "same-race" matching in this larger sample of children of minority ethnicity with adoption recommendations, as we did in the smaller comparison sample. There were again five instances of white English foster carers who had applied to the courts to be adoptive parents of children they had parented for many years. In all the cases, the courts ruled in favour of the foster carers.

There were also 12 cases where there was less emphasis by social workers on "same-race" matching because the children had severe developmental delay or were disabled. For these children, a family that could meet the child's need for physical care and help the child meet their full potential was prioritised. The following extract is about a child with learning difficulties and severe developmental delay:

> . . . *The authority is aware the child is of African/French/British heritage; his cultural identity needs are not being addressed in his current placement. It is, however, felt that of paramount concern at*

---

[27] Promotional activity was not recorded in 25 cases.

this stage of Leo's life is to ensure that his physical care needs are met in order to prevent harm or impairment to his health and/or development. However, Leo's racial and cultural identity will be reinforced to him within his placement, particularly when he gets older. His needs for a positive identity would be assisted by socialisation and life story work, as he gets older. This will need to take into account his ethnic identity as well as his personal and family history which helps build a picture of himself . . . (Social worker's report)

When the ethnicity of the child was unknown, social workers also had fewer reservations about placing children with white adoptive parents. In these circumstances, adopters were needed who could cope with uncertainty, as in the following extract:

[Child's] racial origin is not exactly known and any future adoptive carers will need to be comfortable with this. Future carers will also need to support [the child] around issues of identity and lack of information about her birth father. In the light of the above, I would state that [the child's] needs could be met by white adoptive carers who are comfortable with the above issues.

Prospective adopters

Previous or current foster carers came forward as prospective adopters for a quarter of the children and there were no differences in this regard by ethnicity or authority. This was the same proportion of possible foster-adopters as in the comparison sample.

One or more new adoptive families were considered for 67 per cent of the children.[28] More families came forward for children less than a year old[29] and those featured in family-finding publications.[30] The London borough had used more family-finding promotion and their social

---

[28] Number of potential adopters not recorded for 22 children.
[29] Fisher's Exact p = .001
[30] Fisher's Exact p .0003

workers had a greater choice of families, especially for the mixed ethnicity children, as there were more interested prospective adopters.[31]

Placements at the end of the data collection period

At the end of data collection in 2007, 71 (59%) of the 120 children were in adoptive placements and 15 children (13%) were still waiting for a placement to be found. However, for 34 children (28%), the plan had changed and adoptive parents were no longer being sought. As can be seen in Table 9.3, most Asian children had not been placed for adoption and had a new plan.[32] In contrast, most mixed ethnicity children had found an adoptive family. The three local authorities had taken a similar amount of time to find a placement: from 0–31 months from the date of the panel recommendation for those successfully placed.[33]

Table 9.3
Children's placement outcomes at the end of data collection by ethnicity and local authority (n = 120)

	Child's ethnicity	Placed for aodption	Awaiting an adoptive placement	Change of plan	Total
North	Asian	7	1	5	13
	Mixed	20	4	3	27
Midlands	Black	4	2	0	6
	Asian	1	0	1	2
	Mixed	17	4	7	28
London borough	Black	1	0	5	6
	Asian	1	0	9	10
	Mixed	20	3	5	28

---

[31] Fisher's Exact p = .001

[32] Fisher's Exact p = .001

[33] The time to adoptive placement was zero for the children whose foster carers adopted them

Children who were in adoptive placements at the end of data collection (n = 71)

At the end of data collection, 71 children were in adoptive placements of whom five were black children (42% of all the black children), nine Asian (36% of all the Asian children) and 57 of mixed ethnicity (59% of all the mixed ethnicity children). Most adoptive families had been found in-house and only four children (5%) had been placed through voluntary adoption agencies.

The Asian and black children, for whom adoptive families had been found, were mainly infants, whereas families had been found for older children of mixed ethnicity (see Table 9.4). Even so, most of those placed were very young.

Table 9.4
Mean age in months at the time of the adoption panel for those placed for adoption (n = 71)

	Overall mean	Black (n = 5)	Asian (n = 9)	Mixed (n = 57)
	21	9	7	25
North	18	–	5	22
Midlands	32	10	11	38
London borough	15	3	17	16

Figures 9.1 and 9.2 graphically represents the differences in age between those placed and those where the plan changed. The black bar is the children's average age at the time the panel made the adoption recommendation. The grey bar is the average age of those for whom an adoptive family was found.

The London borough had been slightly less successful at placing its children for adoption, although the differences between local authorities did not reach statistical significance. The Midlands was more successful at family finding for older children than the other two authorities.

123

Figure 9.1

Comparison of adopted and not adopted children's average ages in months at the time the panel made an adoption recommendation

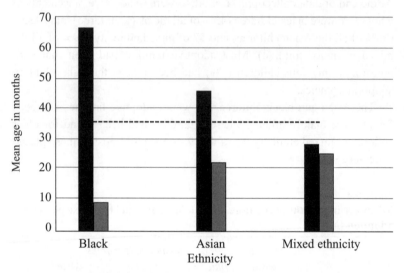

Average age of all the children at panel – Black (n = 12), Asian (n = 25), Mixed ethnicity (n = 83)

Adopted children's age at panel – Black (n = 5), Asian (n = 9), Mixed ethnicity (n = 57)

Age at panel for all children of all ethnicities (n = 120)

Who adopted the children?

Of the 71 children who were in adoptive placements, nearly three-quarters (73%) were placed with new adoptive families, 23 per cent were placed with their previous or present foster carers, and four per cent were placed with kin. Ten per cent of those adopted by "strangers" were adopted by adults who knew the children and were in their networks. For example, one adopter was a child's learning mentor at school.

Most adopters (80%) were heterosexual couples, 17 per cent were single adopters and three per cent were lesbian or gay couples; the London

Figure 9.2

Comparison of children's average ages in months at the time the panel made an adoption recommendation, by local authority and by success of adoption plan

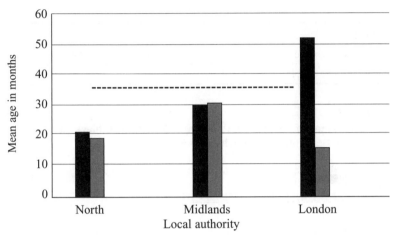

- Age at panel for children by authority – North (n = 40), Midlands (n = 36), London (n = 44)
- Age at panel for children in adoptive placements by authority – North (n = 27), Midlands (n = 22), London (n = 22)
- Age at panel for all children (n = 120)

borough used more diverse adopters[34] than the other two authorities (see Table 9.5).

Ethnically matched adoptive placements

Most of the black and Asian children were in ethnically matched adoptive placements (see Figure 9.3). Black children were better matched in adoptive placements (80% exactly matched) than they had been in foster care placements. Eighty-one per cent of the Muslim and 57 per cent of the

---

[34] Fisher's Exact p = .003

Table 9.5
Characteristics of the adopters in three different authorities (n = 71)

Characteristics of the adopters	North (n = 27) %	Authority Midlands (n = 22) %	London (n = 22) %
Single person	11	4	41
Heterosexual couple	85	96	54
Lesbian or gay couple	4	–	5

Figure 9.3
The percentage of adopters matched by ethnicity with black (n = 5), Asian (n = 9) and mixed ethnicity (n = 57) children

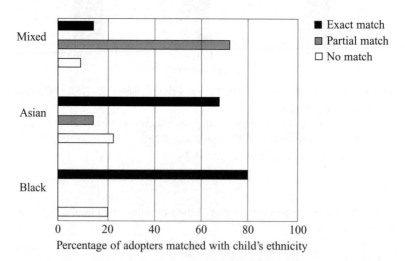

Percentage of adopters matched with child's ethnicity

Christian children were in placements exactly matched by faith and 100 per cent were in placements matched by language. Detailed tables of matches by ethnicity, language and religion are in Appendix II. Although all the Asian children were placed with Asian adopters, the same tendency as seen in the comparison sample was also evident here, with Asian being viewed as an ethnicity in its own right and a failure to distinguish between different heritages.

In seven cases, the children were not matched with any part of their ethnicity, sometimes because of the difficulty of finding adopters to match complex mixed ethnicities. Asian and black adopters also seemed to have more choice in relation to which child to adopt and chose younger children with fewer difficulties.

There were also a few cases where the child's white birth mother did not accept that their mixed ethnicity child was anything other than white. In these situations, social workers were trying to manage the child's future need to understand their diverse heritage, with the birth parent's wish that only a white heritage should be valued, as in the following example:

The birth mother said that the foster carer should ensure that the children only watch and listen to English TV channels. On being reminded that the boys are part Pakistani extract, she pointed out that they are only a quarter Pakistani and that they should not be forced to learn a culture.

In the above example, the social worker went along with the birth mother's wishes (perhaps because religious matching was not sought) and moved the children from their Pakistani Muslim foster carers. The children had spent most of their lives with the foster carers and were settled and used to the foster carers' culture but were moved to a placement with white adopters in a rural environment. File recording suggested that the adoptive placement was not going well and additional support was being planned. In this example, children had been placed without due consideration of their attachments, lived experience of culture, and environment.

The children whose plans had changed by the end of data collection (n = 34)

The 34 children who had their plans changed were five black children (42% of the black children), 15 Asian children (60% of the Asian children) and 14 mixed ethnicity children (17% of the mixed ethnicity children). These children were older on average when they went to panel than the children who were placed for adoption.

Table 9.6

Mean age in months at the time of the adoption panel for the children whose plan to be placed for adoption had changed (n = 34)

		Mean age in months		
	Overall mean	*Black (n = 5)*	*Asian (n = 15)*	*Mixed (n = 14)*
	74	135	73	54
Authority				
North	35	–	41	26
Midlands	38	–	15	42
London borough	104	135	97	85

Why the children's plans changed

Not being able to find suitable adopters was the most common reason recorded for a change of plan away from adoption (see Table 9.7).

Table 9.7

Reasons why the adoption plan had changed (n = 34)

Why the plan changed	*N*	*%*
No adopters meeting social worker's specifications	15	44
Birth family able to provide suitable home	6	18
Decision that present placement is in best interests of the child	8	23
Kin judged able to provide suitable home	4	12
Placement with a family no longer considered[35]	1	3

---

[35] One child was thought to be unsuitable for a family placement because of the severity of her emotional and behavioural difficulties.

It was difficult to be certain from social workers' recording exactly how much effort had been made to find an adoptive family. Some social workers were pessimistic about the likelihood of finding adopters. In a few cases, social workers believed that children were so unlikely to be adopted that they did not pursue necessary court orders or begin family finding. The following example is an extract from the minutes of a panel meeting six months after the initial recommendation.

> *The members added that the child should not be left with the foster carer just because he will be hard to place . . . the members asked the social worker if there had been any efforts to family find. The social worker said 'No'.*

There were also challenges for social workers preferring an Asian family for a mixed ethnicity child of white/Asian heritage. Some Pakistani adopters were not keen to take white/Asian children, as illustrated in this extract from a social worker's case notes.

> *They would only consider if the child "looked like them", meaning they looked Asian and not white. The explanation for this was that they didn't want the child to be rejected by their community [as they had already had so much trouble with the first adopted child].*

And another Pakistani prospective adopter told his or her social worker:

> *. . . these children are seen differently in the Pakistani community . . . people do not accept children of different backgrounds in their families and are treated differently by the wider family and community . . .* (Social worker's notes on Form F)

There were also two examples of adopters who were in a mixed ethnicity relationship who seemed to face some discrimination. For example, a white/Asian couple had been turned down twice for Asian children. They wrote a letter of complaint and in it provided a long list of friends to show how many Asian friends they had. They believed that they had been judged as "not Asian enough".

However, for many children, it was their age that made family finding most difficult, as in the example below.

Illustrative example

The birth mother's ethnicity was described as White/African-Caribbean/Asian and the birth father as white British. The recording in the child's file suggested that the main reasons for difficulties in family finding were complex ethnicity, the child's family history of schizophrenia and his legal status (i.e. lack of Care Order). The review panel noted:

> SW stated she has always been willing to consider any reasonable offers and been flexible about matching considerations. She has considered one Asian family brought up in the Caribbean, one family with an Indian and White member, and one single experienced mother of mixed White/Afro-Caribbean heritage. However, all these families have chosen other children ahead of the child. (Minutes of the review panel)

Placements

Most plans changed to long-term foster care and by the end of data collection the children were in the following placements, as set out in Table 9.8.

Table 9.8
Children's placements at the end of data collection (n = 34)

Children's placements at the end of data collection	*n*	*%*
Local authority long-term foster care	19	56
Returned home	6	17
Independent foster care placement	4	12
Placed with kin/friends	4	12
Residential care (specialist therapeutic)	1	3

Long-term foster care

Social workers were very concerned about ensuring that the child had a stable placement and some plans changed because, after multiple disruptions, the chance of permanence seemed possible when children and foster carers "clicked". In 38 per cent of cases, there was a contingency plan in place to change the plan for adoption if the child was not in an adoptive placement within a stipulated time frame, usually within six to nine months of the adoption recommendation, as in the following example.

Illustrative case example

Two brothers, Jason and Josh, were placed together in foster care with the plan to find adoptive parents who would take both boys. The adoption panel recommended that the workers should only look for a match for up to nine months due to the children's ages and specific behavioural issues. If no placement was found in that time, long-term fostering was to be sought. No adopters came forward after nine months and the plan changed to long-term foster care. At the end of data collection, the brothers had been successfully placed with long-term carers.

Reunifications

It might appear surprising that, after an adoption recommendation, six children returned home. However, these children were being twin-tracked or even triple-tracked, i.e. simultaneously, workers were still considering if reunification was possible while trying to find adopters or long-term foster carers and/or still assessing the possibility of kin placements as in the following example.

Illustrative example

The child, Kylie, was subject to an adoption recommendation but a parallel plan was also put in place for reunification due to the mother's improvement in her mental health. It was agreed to have a further three months to assess the extent of the improvement. The birth mother continued to improve and participated well with Children's Services. Kylie returned to live with her mother in a semi-independent living environment with a high level of support. A full Care Order was in place, so that parental responsibility could be shared with the local authority.

Factors contributing to the final placement outcome

At the end of our data collection, 71 out of the 120 children (59%) were in adoptive placements, 15 (13%) were still awaiting an adoptive placement and 34 children (28%) had had their plans changed away from adoption. It was clear that the child's age was having a major impact on the likelihood of being placed for adoption. We examined how the ages of children at referral, when they first became looked after, and at the time of the panel adoption recommendation affected the final placement outcome (see Figure 9.4 below).

Figure 9.4
Placement outcomes and the children's mean ages at referral, when first looked after and at adoption recommendation (n = 120)

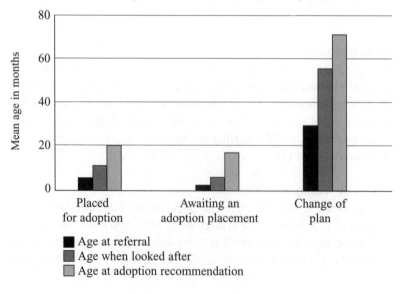

The children who went into the adoptive placements were significantly younger at referral,[36] when first looked after,[37] and at panel,[38] than the children who had their plans changed. Looking at the differences between the authorities, there were no statistical differences in the mean ages of the children in the North and Midlands. However, in the London borough, the children who were in adoptive placements were significantly younger at referral, when first looked after and at panel, when compared to the children whose plans had changed by the end of the data collection period.[39]

Factors contributing to the placement outcome: a model

In the comparison sample, we saw that there were differences in outcome between the white and minority ethnic children. The larger number of minority ethnic children in this sample allowed us to look for differences within the ethnic groups. We wanted to build a statistical model including age and other factors that we thought were contributing to the placement outcome. For analytical purposes, the children's placement outcomes were divided into two categories: the children who were in adoptive placements and the children who were not in adoptive placements by the end of the data collection period. A binary logistic regression was carried out with the child's age at panel, ethnicity, gender, and the local authority as the predictor variables. Although thought to be important, promotion through family-finding publications could not be included as a predictor variable as data for 25 cases were missing. Only the significant predictor variables of age and ethnicity were retained and the coefficients of the final multivariate model are given in Table A4 (see Appendix II).

Reinforcing the results of the comparison sample, the age at panel and the child's ethnicity were significant predictors as to whether the child was in an adoptive placement or not. The odds of being adopted for children who were under a year old at the time of the adoption recommendation were 10 times better than the odds for a child who was more than three

---

[36] Kruskal-Wallis test, p<.001

[37] Kruskal-Wallis test, p<.001

[38] Kruskal-Wallis test, p<.001

[39] Kruskal-Wallis test, p<.001

years in age at panel. Moreover, the odds of being in an adoptive placement for a mixed ethnicity child were four times better than for an Asian child. There were no significant statistical differences between the odds of being adopted for black and mixed ethnicity children.

Time to adoptive placement: a model

In adoption research, establishing the length of time to adoption or change of plan is as important as the factors contributing to the placement outcomes. Being adopted quickly is more desirable than waiting, as we know that the odds of not being adopted increase over time (Selwyn *et al*, 2006). Event history analysis allows modelling of time to an event and the factors that contribute to the outcome. Cox regression, which is an event history method, was conducted to determine whether time to adoptive placement was related to the child's ethnicity, gender, the authority the child came from, and the child's age at panel.

The age of the child at the time of the adoption recommendation was included in the model in the first step and the rest of the variables were included in the second step in a backward elimination procedure to explore the effect of these variables on the outcome. Only those predictors related to the outcome of "time to adoption" were retained and the coefficients of the final multivariate model are given in Table A5 (see Appendix II).

Children who were less than a year old at the time of the adoption recommendation were three times more likely to be adopted *quickly* than the children who were more than three years of age at adoption panel. There was no statistical difference between the children who were aged 0–12 months and 1–3 years at the time the panel met. Figure A2 (see Appendix) gives the model predicted proportions of adopted children by category of the children's age at the time of the adoption recommendation. As can be seen, the model predicts that 50 per cent of the children under a year old at the time the panel meets will be adopted within 10 months of the panel date, and that 50 per cent of the children aged 1–3 years will be adopted within 12 months of the panel.[40]

---

[40] The average time to adoption (median life time) could not be computed for children who were more than three years of age at adoption panel as so few were adopted.

The child's age at the time the panel met (which is invariably linked with age at referral and age when first looked after) and their ethnicity are factors that predict whether a child will be adopted or not. In effect, this means that younger children and mixed ethnicity children have better odds of being adopted. Moreover, the final Cox regression revealed that young children are more likely to be adopted quickly than those who are older at panel. However, it should be noted that, although all statistical analyses were conducted stringently and all requirements met, these results should be interpreted in the light of the unequal numbers of minority ethnic children within our sample, with 69 per cent of the 120 children being of mixed ethnicity and only 10 per cent black and 21 per cent Asian.

Summary

- The children were looked after for, on average, 10 months before an adoption recommendation was made. Half the children were under 15 months of age at the time the panel met to make a recommendation for adoption. Black and Asian children waited longer in care before a recommendation was made.
- Promotion through family-finding publications was used for half the children, but the likelihood of being promoted was not associated with age, extent of special needs or gender. The London borough used more promotion than the other two authorities and this resulted in significantly more prospective adopters to choose from.
- At the end of data collection, 59 per cent of the children were in adoptive placements, 13 per cent were waiting for a placement and for 28 per cent the plan had changed away from adoption.
- The time it took to find an adoptive placement ranged from 0–31 months and most children were in placements exactly or partially matched by ethnicity.
- Most mixed ethnicity children had been found an adoptive family while most Asian children had not. Only very young black and Asian children had been placed. Changes to the adoption plan occurred on average 14 months after the recommendation, usually because no suitable adopter could be found.

- The child's age (at the time the panel met) and their ethnicity were significant predictors of whether a child was or was not in an adoptive placement. Infants were ten times more likely to be adopted than a child older than three years and mixed ethnicity children were four times more likely to be adopted than Asian children.
- The child's age was the only significant predictor of time to adoption. Children who were infants at the time of the adoption panel were placed much more speedily than older children.
- The child's age at the time of the adoption recommendation was associated with their age at referral, length of time looked after before the panel made its recommendation, and the social worker's practice.

10 Children recommended for adoption: white and minority ethnic children compared

In this chapter, we make some comparisons between white and minority ethnic children. The adoption recommended sample deliberately selected only minority ethnic children, so that we could obtain a larger sample. However, some comparisons with white children are possible, if the white children with adoption recommendations from the comparison sample (Chapters 3–6) are added to the minority ethnic children from the adoption recommended sample. Therefore, the data in this chapter reflect differences between white and minority ethnic children who went to panel and where all had adoption recommendations.

Our focus is on the characteristics of the children and the parents, the reasons for the decision to recommend adoption, and the quality of the information used in that decision. In addition, we look at any differences in the ways in which the children were "processed", that is, for any evidence of differential decision making and service provision. The purpose of this chapter is not to repeat all the analyses already conducted on the adoption recommended and comparison samples, but to look at important contrasts between white and minority ethnic children.

The sample

The samples in these analyses are the 36 white children with adoption recommendations from the comparison sample and 120 minority ethnic children from the adoption recommended sample. The sampling approach and data collection procedures for all these children were the same. The analyses concerning the children use all the children in each group, including those who were siblings, but data on parents and families are based on numbers of parents, not numbers of children.

Background and demographic characteristics

The children

Key comparative data on the children with adoption recommendations are given in Table 10.1.

Table 10.1
Children's characteristics and experiences

	White (n = 36) %	Black (n = 12) %	Asian (n = 25) %	Mixed (n = 83) %
Boys	56	25	48	54
Abandoned/relinquished	8	17	28	7
Child with FASD or drug withdrawal	8	8	8	30*
On CPR	51	33	52	69
On CPR – neglect	47	17*	44	61
On CPR – other abuse	11	17	8	7
	Mean (SD)	Mean (SD)	Mean (SD)	Mean (SD)
Age at first Children's Services involvement (months)	7.8 (16.1)	41.58 (59.5)	16.00 (34.2)	6.51 (15.2)
Age first looked after (months)	19.4 (22.0)	50.75 (61.3)	33.2 (44.1)	19.20 (26.0)
Age at adoption recommendation (months)	26.9 (24.9)	65.9 (64.5)	46.4 (50.9)	28.1 (29.9)

* Significantly different from the other groups: comparison of adjusted standardised residuals

As can be seen, the black group contained fewer boys than the white, Asian or mixed ethnicity groups, and the black children were, on average, older when Children's Services first became involved with them.

Table 10.2
Mothers' ethnicity and characteristics

Characteristic	White (n = 69–71) %	Black (n = 11–14) %	Asian (n = 17) %	Mixed ethnicity (n = 17–18) %	Statistical difference
Ever in care	36	15	0	78	p = 0.000+
Abused or neglected	62	38	20	83	p = 0.001+
Children already removed to care or adopted	51	43	41	56	ns
Any relinquished or concealed children	11	14	41*	6	p = 0.022
Child with FASD/drug withdrawal symptoms	21	14	12	44*	p = 0.03
Has a partner at home	13	14	29	6	ns
Domestic violence	49	21	41	39	ns
Maternal alcohol/substance abuse	57	36	6	78	p = 0.000
Maternal history of violence or imprisonment	52	43	20	61	p = 0.08

Mothers' ethnicity (column group header)

* Significantly different from the other groups combined.
+ Significance explained by the high rates in the mixed group and the low rates amongst Asian mothers (adjusted residuals)

139

Consequently, they were also older when they were first looked after and when the recommendation for adoption was made. This small group is distinctly different from the other three.

Child protection registrations (CPR) were higher for the mixed ethnicity children, for whom registrations for neglect were much more common. The mixed ethnicity children also had a significantly higher rate of FASD or neo-natal abstinence syndrome noticed at or shortly after birth.

The mothers

Analyses of parental characteristics were straightforward for mothers but not for fathers, since children in the same sibling group often had different fathers, as shown in previous chapters. Here we focus only on the mothers (Table 10.2) – sample sizes vary because of missing information in children's files. When reading this table, it is important to remember that white mothers were the mothers of about half the minority ethnic children. For example, the column headed "White" includes the white mothers of the white children and the white mothers of mixed ethnicity children.

There were no significant differences in the age of mothers when Children's Services became involved: most mothers were in their mid-twenties. Although more Asian mothers had a partner, this did not reach statistical significance nor did being subject to domestic violence, the rate of which was high overall. However, Asian mothers were significantly more likely to have relinquished a child, and mothers, who themselves were of mixed ethnicity, to have a child with FASD or affected by drugs. Indeed, the childhood experiences and adult difficulties for this group of mothers are very striking and show up the failures of social provision and support when the mothers in this group were children.

Further comparisons of mothers' characteristics are useful: that between the white mothers of white children and the white mothers of minority ethnic children. These comparisons are given in Table 10.3.

The two groups of women did not differ on most characteristics and experiences, although the childhoods of the white mothers of minority ethnic children were somewhat more adverse. They were also less likely

Table 10.3
Characteristics of white mothers according to child's ethnicity

	White mothers with white children (n = 32)*	White mothers with minority ethnic children (n = 39)	Statistical difference
Mother's age at Children's Services involvement	26.28 (7.1)	26.21 (6.91)	ns
	%	%	
Ever in care	28	42	ns
Abused or neglected	61	67	ns
Children already removed to care or adopted	50	51	ns
Any relinquished or concealed children	9	13	ns
Child with FASD/drug withdrawal symptoms	9	31	p = 0.04
Has a partner at home	41	13	p = 0.013
Domestic violence	41	54	ns
Alcohol/substance misuse	45	67	p = 0.064
History of violence or imprisonment	45	57	ns

* Numbers in each analysis vary slightly because of missing data.

to have a partner and more likely to misuse alcohol or drugs. Consequently, they were significantly more likely to have children who were born with symptoms of FASD or neo-natal abstinence syndrome.

Reasons for becoming looked after and care history

Here, we look briefly at how the families became the focus of sustained interest to Children's Services, what happened subsequently, and whether there were ethnic differences in this. As we have shown in previous chapters, the black children were on average older than the children of white, Asian or mixed ethnicity at the point of sustained Children's Services involvement.

Sources of referral

There were statistically significant differences in the sources of referral at the start of sustained social work intervention. The most usual source of referral was community child health services but a higher proportion of white children were referred by Children's Services and a higher proportion of black and Asian children by education services or by their own families.

Reasons for referral

There were also differences in the reason that led to the referral. The great majority of all children, regardless of ethnicity, became of concern because of abuse or neglect. Significantly, fewer black *mothers* were referred for child neglect than the other three groups, but this might have been because of the older age of the black children at referral. Mothers who were themselves of mixed ethnicity were most likely to be referred for neglect although this did not quite reach statistical significance.

Number of placements and the timing of events

We checked whether there were any ethnic differences in the stability of placements, the length of the time between first episode of Children's Services involvement and becoming looked after, and then between both of these variables and the length of time to an adoption recommendation. We look later at the likelihood of a recommendation resulting in an adoptive placement and how long this took. The data on placements and on the timing of the earlier phases are given in Table 10.4.

There were no significant differences between the groups on the length of time between the referral and becoming looked after, nor on the length of time from being looked after to an adoption being recommended, nor on the number of foster placements or the number of kinship placements. Since most of the children had only one foster placement, we

Table 10.4
Placement history and timing

	White (n = 36) (SD)	Black (n = 12) (SD)	Asian (n = 25) (SD)	Mixed (n = 83) (SD)
Mean months from referral to becoming looked after	11.6 (17.8)	9.2 (24.0)	17.2 (29.3)	12.7 (21.1)
Mean months from becoming looked after to adoption recommendation	7.5 (4.6)	14.1 (8.96)	12.8 (9.7)	9.3 (8.3)
Number of all placements	1.7 (1.0)	2.3 (1.7)	1.8 (1.4)	1.7 (1.0)
Foster placements (LA & IFA)	1.4 (0.5)	1.7 (1.1)	1.5 (1.1)	1.5 (0.9)
Number with kin placements	2	0	4	12

checked whether there were differences on the proportions with more than one, but there were not.

Possible delays in care history prior to going to panel

Since there were some differences in the length of time children were looked after before an adoption recommendation was made, even though these were not statistically significant, it is worth exploring why this might have been so and whether it was evidence of delay. The Asian and black children spent longer in this phase than the white children or those of mixed ethnicity. We rated delay if there was a lack of permanency planning after a child had been looked after for four months. The ethnic differences on this rating were striking.

Permanency planning was significantly more often delayed for children of black or Asian ethnicity. A possible reason for delay was that the families of the white and mixed ethnicity children were more often

Table 10.5
Delay in permanency planning after children became looked after

	White (n = 36) %	Black (n = 12) %	Asian (n = 25) %	Mixed (n = 83) %
No delay	75	25	36	64
Delay	25	75	64	36

$p = 0.001$, significantly less delay for white and mixed ethnicity children

known to Children's Services, and therefore that decisions and speed were shaped by previous experiences with the family. Current referrals were made against a history of previous referrals or work with the family for 80 per cent of white mothers, 43 per cent of black mothers, 53 per cent of Asian mothers and 61 per cent of mothers of mixed ethnicity ($p = 0.01$). Overall, delay was significantly more likely if the family was new to Children's Services. We examine later whether delays occurred during the process of adoption itself.

Planning

Other possible indicators of differences in the service response to children of different ethnicities are the quality of planning and changes in plans as the children moved towards permanence. The plans for children of all ethnicities when they first became looked after were predominantly for return home within six months or for adoption.[41] All other kinds of plans – for example, long-term foster or kinship care – applied to only a very small proportion of children in any group.

The quality of information and assessments

Good planning and the adequate matching of children's needs to adopters' capacities are not possible without good assessments. Many studies have highlighted the importance of good information in the adoption process

---

[41]   *Return home*: White children 47%, Black 50%, Asian 48%, Mixed 31%
   adoption: White children 47%, Black 25%, Asian 40% and Mixed 57%

Table 10.6
Quality of information and assessments

	White (n = 36) %	Black (n = 12) %	Asian (n = 25) %	Mixed (n = 83) %	Statistical difference
Completed core assessment	50	25	36	57	p = 0.002
Adequate or detailed Form E	58	60	55	42	ns
Adoption medical	78	64	36	73	p = 0.003
Health plan	72	42	20	51	p = 0.001
Education plan	100*(8)+	80 (5)	33 (9)	53 (19)	p = 0.017
Chronology	75	67	60	78	ns
Change in adoption plan before any placement	17	42	60	17	p = 0.000

* missing Form E for three white, two black, three Asian and 11 mixed ethnicity children
+ figures in brackets are the numbers of eligible children

and its frequent lack in practice. Here we look for any differences between children of different ethnicities and the quality of information and of assessments of children by the time the recommendation for adoption was made and between that time and the end of data collection. Some key indicators are set out in Table 10.6.

Completed core assessments were less common for black and Asian children, although there were fewer differences if partially completed assessments were also included.[42] Nevertheless, the frequent lack of these assessments for all groups is disturbing. This was also the case for adequate or detailed Form Es, where the lack of good-quality assessments was apparent for all groups of children regardless of ethnicity.

---

[42] 58% White, 75% Black, 44% Asian, 75% Mixed

Chronologies were more frequently present, although these were missing for between a fifth and a third of children.

There were significant differences according to ethnicity on whether an adoption medical had been done, whether there was a health plan and an education plan. These three assessments were all significantly more likely to be present for the white children, although assessments were often missing for them as well.

Finally, the black and Asian children were much more likely to have had their plans changed from adoption to some other form of placement, whereas children of mixed ethnicity were similar to the white children in terms of likelihood that the adoption plan would be taken forward.

Agencies involved in assessments

Table 10.7 shows the agencies involved in assessments. There were no significant differences in the involvement of GPs, health visitors, early years services, or probation, and no differences in the average number of services involved in the assessment of children in each ethnic group. However, there were differences in the involvement of nursery schools (less frequent for white children), adult mental health services (more frequent for the parents of black and Asian children), family centres (more frequent for children of mixed ethnicity) and other services, such as housing, which were more frequent for white children.

The difference in the involvement of adult mental health services in the assessments of the children clearly reflects the influence of individual parents on the figures. The difference disappears if the analysis is based on mothers rather than children. Nevertheless, the remarkably low involvement of adult mental health services with the assessment of mothers with alcohol or drug problems is very worrying – they were involved in assessments of families for only six of the 61 mothers (10%) with such problems.

The outcome of adoption panel recommendations

For some children, the plan for adoption changed to another form of plan before any placements were made, with more changes away from adoption for the children of black and Asian ethnicity, significantly so for the

Table 10.7
Agencies involved in initial or core assessments of children

	White (n = 36) %	Black (n = 12) %	Asian (n = 25) %	Mixed (n = 83) %	Statistical difference
GP	28	33	36	35	ns
Health visitors	56	58	20	62	p = 0.002
Early years	8	25	4	14	ns
Nursery or school	11	25	24	29	ns
Child mental health	6	8	12	11	ns
Adult mental health	14	17	20	5	ns
Probation	6	17	4	9	ns
Family centre	25	8	20	40	ns
Other	53	8	28	35	p = 0.029
Average number of services	2.1 (1.3)	2.0 (1.4)	1.68 (1.8)	2.3 (1.6)	ns

latter. The differences were almost entirely accounted for by the failure to find suitable adopters for these children or by a decision that their current non-adoptive placement was in their best interests (Table 10.8). These issues for the minority ethnic children were explored in the previous chapter.

Promotion through family-finding publications

The differences between ethnicities in the frequency with which plans were changed might have been linked to uncertainty about what to do and consequent differences in the amount of effort put into family finding. One possible indicator of this was the use of promotion in trying to find placements for the children. Differences in this were noted in the previous chapter. For over one-quarter (27%) of the children, there was no information on file on whether promotion had been used or considered. It is likely that these children were not promoted, since promotion incurs costs and

Table 10.8
Reasons why plans were changed

	White (n = 6)	Black (n = 5)	Asian (n = 15)	Mixed (n = 14)
Reason for change not known	1	0	5	1
Current non-adoptive placement in child's best interests	3	2	3	1
No adopters meeting social worker's specifications	1	2	3	6
Birth family or kin judged able to provide a suitable home	1	0	4	6
Placement with family no longer considered	0	1	0	0

The black and Asian children had their plans changed significantly more than the white and mixed ethnicity children.

these are usually recorded. Table 10.9 gives the proportions of those with different ethnicities who were promoted, assuming that those with missing data were not.

As can be seen, promotion was used more often for mixed ethnicity children and least for the white children, but it was also used least for those children whose plans went on to change.

Contact after the adoption recommendation

Children's Services are expected to promote contact between children and birth parents, unless there are good reasons against it. Table 10.10 shows whether contact actually occurred with the birth mother and the birth father, and sets this against the expectations in the contact plan. Plans for

Table 10.9

Percentages of children promoted through family-finding publications

	White (n = 36) %	Black (n = 12) %	Asian (n = 25) %	Mixed (n = 83) %
Not promoted+	83	75	72	54
Promoted once	14	8	28	35
Promoted more than once	3	17	0	11

p = 0.016 exact test.

+ Includes those for whom there was no information on the file

Table: 10.10

Contact with birth parents between the adoption recommendation and the end of data collection

	White (n = 33) %	Black (n = 10)[43] %	Asian (n = 25) %	Mixed (n = 83) %
Contact with mother				
Actual	70	20*	60	49
Planned	100	75	88	84
Contact with father				
Actual	31	0*	32	22
Planned	55	60	69	52

*Contact with mother and father was significantly different for the black group (adjusted standardised residuals).

contact with birth fathers were less optimistic and were often not achieved even so.

Contact with birth mothers was planned for all the white children and the majority of minority ethnic children as well. However, these plans came to fruition quite variably for the different ethnic groups. Contact

[43] Data missing for two cases

with mother was highest for the white children (as planned) and lowest for the black children, despite a fairly high level of expectation.

Placements by the end of data collection

Finally, in this brief comparative chapter, we look at where the children were placed by the time the case file data collection finished; the data are given in Table 10.11. Differences between minority ethnic children have been discussed in the previous chapters. Here we look at the significant differences between them and the white children.

Table 10.11
Placement outcomes for the children at the end of data collection

	White (n = 36) %	Black (n = 12) %	Asian (n = 25) %	Mixed (n = 83) %
In an adoptive placement	83	42	36	69
Awaiting an adoptive placement	0	16	4	14
Plan changed	17	42	60	17

P = 0.00 significance accounted for by the proportion of Asian children no longer seeking adoptive placements and the lack of white children waiting.

The more frequent changes in plans for the black and Asian children have already been commented on. The difference between them and the white and mixed ethnicity children is striking.

Multivariate analyses

Here we repeat the analyses (see Chapter 9) of the predicted time to and probability of adoption using a Cox proportional hazards analysis. That analysis showed that minority ethnic children, who were under a year old at the time of the adoption recommendation, were adopted more quickly than the children who were older than three years.

In this analysis, we add the 36 white children who have featured in the analyses in this chapter. Age at panel, ethnicity, local authority area and the gender of the child were included as the predictor variables in the model. By adding white children to the model, ethnicity as well as age became a significant predictor of time to adoption. The coefficients of the final multivariate model are given in Table A6 (see Appendix II).

The results confirm what we already know from the analyses of the adoption recommended sample: that the children who were less than a year old at panel were more likely to have an adoptive placement and to be placed more quickly. However, in this model, both age categories were significant in comparison with the reference group (children 0–1 years old). Similarly, using white children as the reference group, black and Asian children had less probability of being adopted but there were no significant differences between the white and mixed ethnicity children.

Figure A3 (see Appendix II) gives the predicted proportions of children adopted according to the children's age at the time of the adoption recommendation. As can be seen, the model predicts that, of the children who have panel recommendation for adoption:

- 50 per cent of white and minority ethnic children under 12 months of age will be adopted within eight months;
- 50 per cent of white and minority ethnic children aged between one and three years will be adopted within 12 months;
- 50 per cent of white and minority ethnic children who are older than three years will be adopted within 19 months of the adoption recommendation.

Figure A4 (see Appendix II) gives the predicted time to adoption for children of different ethnicities. As can be seen, the white children are the quickest to be adopted with 50 per cent being adopted within 10 months of the adoption recommendation, compared with the 12, 16 and 19 months for the mixed ethnicity, Asian and black children. These predictions for the different ethnicities take into account differences in age at the time the panel.

The data on the children recommended for adoption in this and the previous two chapters show clearly the complexities of individual cases and the decisions made about them. In the last section of this report we turn to the prospective or real-time study of a new sample of 50 children, whose progress towards permanence was tracked through monthly interviews with social workers from just before the first meeting of the panel until our study ended in summer 2007.

Summary

- The small group of black children were distinctly different from the children of white, Asian or mixed ethnicity. There were few significant differences except that more Asian children had been relinquished and more mixed ethnicity children had been on the Child Protection Register, especially for neglect.
- There were no differences between mothers on their age when they came to the notice of Children's Services. However, Asian mothers were significantly more likely to have relinquished their children.
- The characteristics of white mothers of white children and white mothers of mixed ethnicity children were generally similar, although the latter were much less likely to have a partner at home and much more likely to misuse substances and to have a child with FASD or neo-natal abstinence syndrome.
- Community child health services were the most frequent referral agencies. Black and Asian children were more likely to be referred by education services or by their own families.
- There were no significant differences in the length of time between first concern and becoming looked after or in the number of foster placements.
- There was significantly less delay in permanency planning for the white and mixed ethnicity children. This was associated with a greater likelihood that their families were already known to Children's Services.
- Lack of core assessments were common for all children but significantly more so for black and Asian children. An adoption medical, a health plan and an education plan were significantly more likely to be present for white children.
- There were significantly more changes in the plan away from adoption

for black and Asian children and for the plan to be changed more quickly.
- The likelihood of adoption was significantly higher for white children and for infants of all ethnicities.

Interviews with
social workers

11 Interviews with social workers

The sample of children and their social workers was obtained by asking the adoption panel administrators in our three local authorities to identify minority ethnic children who had been "booked" into panel to be considered for a "should be placed for adoption" recommendation. We decided to select only one child per family if a sibling group had been booked into panel, as we wanted to maximise the number of children and social workers in the sample. In total, 50 children met the sample criteria between November 2005 and December 2006. The children's files were read and data collected from their files in the same way as in the other two samples.

The 50 children had 49 social workers – two children were on one social worker's caseload. Social workers were interviewed face-to-face just before the panel met and, from then on, monthly telephone calls were made to the social worker until the child was placed or data collection ceased in December 2006. Social workers were asked about family finding, decision-making, placements, and adoption support. A final telephone call was made in July/August 2007 to find out if the child had been placed for adoption or if there had been any changes to the plan.

The social workers

The social workers were mainly female (43) and there were slightly more white social workers than social workers of a minority ethnicity (see Table 11.1).

We asked the social workers how many times they had previously been to a panel meeting in order to get some indication of their familiarity with adoption processes. Fifteen workers were very experienced and had been to panel on at least ten previous occasions, 29 had been to panel more than once and six workers had never been to panel.

Table 11.1
Ethnicity of the children and their social workers

Children's ethnicity	Social worker's ethnicity				
	White	*Black*	*Asian*	*Mixed*	*Total*
Black	1	1			2
Asian	5	4	1	1	11
Mixed	21	8	5	3	37
Total	**27**	**13**	**6**	**4**	**50**

Children's social workers' views and opinions about adoption and permanency

On being asked what they thought the key problems were in finding adoption placements for minority ethnic children, social workers spoke of complex and overlapping reasons connected with the child, the agency and the prospective adopters.

Just over a third of workers talked about the shortage of adopters, especially for Asian, mixed ethnicity children and for minority ethnic children with a disability. None linked the shortage with population demographics but described other reasons. Some thought there was reluctance in the general population to become involved with Children's Services and that a child's characteristics, such as having an uncertain or uncommon ethnicity, behavioural and developmental concerns, or the need to place outside the local community, made it difficult to recruit adopters. Social workers thought that adoption procedures and regulations particularly deterred minority ethnic adopters, and that Eurocentric assessments and current recruitment techniques reflected a lack of sensitivity to "race" and ethnicity issues. Class and economic issues were also raised as factors, which prevented minority ethnic adults from becoming adoptive parents. Individuals within minority ethnic communities were described as having a different cultural understanding of adoption and saw it as a more informal arrangement, as in the following interview extract:

The main problem is that a lot of Asian and African families view adoption as different. Sometimes they consider adoption as a more private fostering arrangement. Sometimes within their own family networks they take children in without any formal arrangement. So a lot of them struggle with our . . . rules and regulations and everything being permanent . . . Quite possibly also, a lot of African and Asian people . . . don't have the time and energy to put themselves forward, because they are taking in children on an informal basis. These are vast generalisations but these are some of the factors why people are not coming forward to be adopters.

We asked what could be done to increase the number of minority ethnic adopters. Social workers suggested greater promotion of adoption by talking with existing community and women's groups about the reality of adoption; advertising in community languages; more targeted recruitment activities in community venues; trying to change attitudes to adoption; using more minority ethnic adopters and workers in recruitment and training; increasing the availability of adoption allowances; and having a greater diversity of people on the adoption panel and in family-finding teams.

Social workers were asked if they thought that finding an ethnically matched adoptive placement was more likely to be achieved for some ethnic groups rather than others. Although 26 per cent of the social workers thought there was no difference, over half (54%) said that better matching outcomes were achieved for white children. Moreover, three-quarters thought that adoption was more likely to be achieved for white children.

The use of targets in adoption
Two-thirds of social workers stated that targets had led to increased work pressure. These pressures were seen as coming from senior managers (30%), line managers (24%), performance management staff (14%) and "other" sources (8%) such as from the courts and the increasing amounts of administrative paperwork that had to be completed to deadlines. While some viewed the targets as unrealistic and unachievable, others thought they were useful.

Long-term foster care

Social workers were asked to voice their thoughts about long-term foster-ing as a permanency option for minority ethnic children. The majority (68%) thought it was the best option for older children and a few workers (8%) thought long-term foster carers were better able to meet children's cultural needs than were adopters. Two workers thought there was a greater chance of siblings being placed together in foster care and that contact arrangements were smoother. However, nine workers also described it as unstable and unable to offer a permanent home and family for children.

The children's characteristics

There were no sibling groups in this sample because of our sampling criteria. However, most of the children (70%) had siblings and just as in the previous samples, a large number (40%) had siblings who were of a different ethnicity. There were slightly more girls (52%) than boys (48%) and the majority of the children were from the Northern authority (see Table 11.2).

The majority (74%) of children were again of mixed ethnicity, with fewer Asian (22%) and very few black (4%) children. Forty per cent of the children were Muslim, 18 per cent Christian, and two per cent Rastafarian, while 12 per cent had no religion.[44] English was the language spoken in most family homes (82%) with a few children speaking Sylheti

Table 11.2
Children's ethnicity and local authority

	Black *(n = 2)*	*Asian* *(n = 11)*	*Mixed* *(n = 37)*
North	1	4	21
Midlands		0	9
London borough	1	7	7

---

[44] The child's religion was not recorded in 28 per cent of cases.

(10%), Punjabi (4%), Somali (2%) or French (2%). All but two children were UK nationals.

At the time of the first interview with the child's social workers, the children's average age was just over 19 months old (Figure 11.1) and only four (8%) were of school age. Black children were, on average, older than Asian or mixed ethnicity children and, as with the other samples in this study, the children from the London borough were older, although the differences between authorities were not statistically significant. Data from the children's files showed that the children had very low levels of special needs identified on the Form E. Ten (20%) children had neo-natal abstinence syndrome reported at birth and there were concerns about the development of seven other children, including one child who had a physical disability.

Social worker's length of involvement with the child

The majority of social workers had not known the child for very long – eight months on average with over a third of workers (38%) heaving met the child in the previous month. We asked if the child had had the same

Figure 11.1
Box plot of children's ages at interview by ethnicity

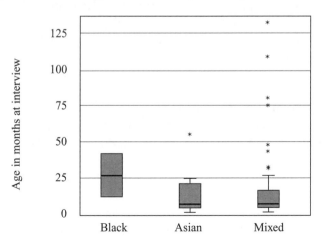

worker since Children's Services became involved and only eight (16%) children had had no change of worker. We were also interested to know whether there were plans to change the social worker again once the adoption recommendation was made, perhaps because responsibility passed to another team. However, 78 per cent of social workers said they expected to continue working with the child and intended to see them into their adoptive placements. Social workers stated that they visited the child at least monthly, with 42 per cent visiting the child every week or fortnight.

Knowledge of the child's temperament and needs

We knew that the social worker would be expected, when presenting the child's case to the panel, to be able to answer questions about the child's characteristics, personality, and needs. Many of the children in the sample were infants and we used the well-known Thomas and Chess (1977) dimensions to ask about the infants' characteristics.

Although a third of workers had only recently met the child, they all thought they had a good understanding of the child's needs. Most of the babies or infants were described as happy and contented, easily com- forted, sleeping well and with no particular developmental difficulties. Four children were described as having characteristics that fitted the "slow to warm up and difficult to engage" category, and three were said to be very difficult, poor sleepers and irritable. Fifteen children had some difficulties in feeding or eating, with one child's problems being described as severe. Social workers thought they had good relationships with the children, although one worker could not answer questions about whether the child had a best friend, a pet, or had any likes and dislikes.

The child's current placement

Social workers were asked about whether they thought the child's experience of being looked after had been generally positive. The majority (81%) thought it had been a good or very good experience, 17 per cent a mixed or variable experience, and for one child (2%) the experience had been very poor.

There had been a choice of foster placements for the majority of children at the time they first became looked after. Seven children had

Table 11.3
Children's placement at the time of the social work interview

	Number of children
Local authority foster carers	44
IFP placement	3
Kinship care placement	1
Newborn baby in hospital	1
Residential parent/baby assessment unit	1

been in emergency placements and a further 17 children had been placed where there was a vacancy. At the time of our interviews, just over half (26) the children were living with white foster carers and most of these were mixed ethnicity children. All the Asian children were with Asian foster carers (in two cases not an exact match), and one of the two black children was placed with a black foster carer.

Planning for adoption

Most social workers had no reservations about the making of an adoption plan and thought it was in the best interests of the child. About a third (32%), while agreeing that adoption should be in the plan, also expressed sadness, and said they always found the adoption decision difficult. The parents' inability to make the necessary changes, the child's young age and a lack of suitable kin as alternative carers were all mentioned as reasons for choosing adoption. Departmental policy and national adoption targets were not mentioned as factors that had influenced the making of an adoption plan.

For 33 (66%) of the children, no other option but adoption was being pursued. Kinship care was still being explored for seven children (14%) and reunification with the birth family was being considered for ten (20%). Fourteen (26%) of the children had siblings who were also being considered for adoption by the panel. The plans were to place six of the sample children separately from their siblings, whilst the social workers hoped to find placements for two sample children with their whole sibling group, and six with some of their siblings.

Foster carers applying to adopt

Social workers stated that the majority (77%) of foster carers had not shown any interest in being considered as prospective adopters for the child. In most cases, social workers thought this was because foster carers did not want to change their role, although a few (3) also thought that lower adoption allowances had deterred them.

Foster carers' applications to adopt were being supported by the local authority in relation to eight (17%) children. A further three foster carers had asked about adoption, but they had not been encouraged to make an application. The reasons given for considering the carers unsuitable were because they were not culturally matched, or they appeared not to understand the difference between fostering and adoption, or because adopters were needed who would take the whole sibling group.

Delays in permanency planning

Social workers were asked whether they thought there had been any delay in planning for the children. Workers described delay for 22 (44%) children and attributed this mainly to staff shortages and a failure to implement the care plan. Slow legal proceedings and late applications made by kin were also given as reasons for delay.

Support and training for social workers

None of the social workers had received any external support or advice (for example, from BAAF consultants) around ethnicity and culture when making the adoption decision for the child. Several viewed this as something that would be relevant later on and one social worker said:

> *I think that's going to come ... If they are approved for adoption, it's going to be hard to identify a family that's going to meet her ethnic needs, in particular, because there's a bit of Italian there as well ... Would she be better with an Asian family or an English family? I don't know.*

However, 12 workers mentioned previous training, guidance, and support that they had found helpful and could draw upon in thinking about the planning they had to do now, as described below:

> ... I did attend 'Working with Bangladeshi children and families', so that was a very, very good training. You understood the history of why Bengalis came here, the different language ... how the Bengali family systems work ... It was a two-day training but it was enough to assist me in my thinking and my way of preparation for [child], just understanding his family's background ...

Seven social workers mentioned help and advice from managers and other local authority social work staff. Three workers got support from a panel run by the local authority that provided advice on minority ethnic children's needs, as explained in the interview extract below:

> It's a panel and you're invited to take any cases where there's black or dual heritage children if you're unsure about what to do with the case, whether it's adoption, fostering, just general child protection, anything really ... I'm actually going tomorrow afternoon just to kind of seek their views on appropriateness in terms of placement and such like.

The children's birth parents

Nearly half of the children's mothers were white (48%): a similar proportion to that found in our other samples. Most parents (78%) were said by the social worker to be still contesting the adoption plan and, where this was the case, relatives too were often objecting. Five birth mothers (10%) had relinquished the child, and a further six (12%) supported the local authority adoption plan.

Collecting information on the child's family

The Form E[45] requires social workers to provide information on the culture, religion, language, identity, and background of the child's mother

---

[45] Now the Child's Permanence Report

165

and father and to record the parent's own views about the kind of adoptive family they would wish for their child. Social workers were asked what had helped them to talk about these issues with the birth parents. Most drew on work experiences and a few mentioned training courses they had attended and supportive colleagues, and five mentioned the importance of supervision. A few white workers (3) stated that having a minority ethnic partner or knowledge gained from their degree courses or being a mother of mixed parentage children had helped them to communicate with parents. Many talked of a combination of factors that had helped, as in the following extract:

> In this team we are trained extensively and I've had years of experience working with child rights issues and many, many years of working ... We have a lot of professional meetings ... We really do encourage partnership between the client as well as us ... So it's a lot of information which I have at hand, coupled with the supervision, training, the meetings, the feedback, information, experience, and talking with colleagues, etc, so everything combined together is important.

Several social workers spoke about the good working relationship they had with the birth parents. This was attributed to being able to speak to the mother in her first language, or being able to explain the local authority's "same-race" placement policy, or being able to give information about the adoptive family to the birth mother. Social workers of minority ethnicity also said they drew on their own life experiences and some (16%) described their own ethnicity and culture as very important factors in talking to birth parents, as expressed in the following extracts:

> ... being Asian, I know how important it is to know about your culture, to know about your identity and to know where you've come from, so as a Black worker, I'm able to take that into account when I work with any child, regardless of race ...

> ... I think one of the things that was most profound in getting them to talk to me is the fact that I could relate to them, because they have had to integrate into this community in the same way that I have had to

integrate in this community. So I think that was something that was similar for us both.

However, a few workers (4) were reluctant to talk to birth parents because reunification was still a possibility or Care Orders had not been granted and the timing was considered wrong. Some workers only asked the parent(s) once about their views and, if the parents refused to answer questions, they were not asked again. Others assumed that the birth mother and father shared the same culture, and differences between them were not clarified. A few (4) thought that the parents' views on "matching" in adoptive placements would be similar to the views parents had expressed about foster placements, as in the extract below.

Father's views would be that he would want him to be placed with Indian people, and mother's views would be that she would want them placed with white people who had some "Indian influence", quote unquote. That would be their views because their general comments about foster carers . . . have been along those lines, and they would have similar views, I presume, for what they wanted for adopters. But they haven't said that, because they don't want to talk about adoption.

Social workers were asked whether they felt comfortable asking questions about parental culture, religion, and identity. Most (82%) thought they had no difficulty in asking such questions, but it was the parents who refused to co-operate and give the information. Workers thought that parental refusal to co-operate was the main reason for gaps in information on children's files. Social workers said that, because many parents were contesting the adoption, they were not ready to co-operate, as this would imply that they were accepting of the adoption decision, as they explained below.

I have a very difficult relationship with mum . . . She doesn't want to have any in-depth discussion about adoption at all because she's completely not in agreement with it and her view is he should be returned home, so she's not actually at a stage where she's prepared to give any consideration to where he'd be best placed . . .

Because, like I said, birth mother . . . most of the time she's not available. When you organise a meeting with her, she doesn't turn up and you can't contact her, she doesn't take mobile phones, you don't know where she is living, we write letters to her place, she doesn't respond and visit, she's not there. It's difficult with mum.

Surprisingly, none of the social workers referred to there being an independent support worker for either the mother or father of the child, although a support worker might have helped to engage the birth parents and to gather information about their background and their wishes with regard to matching. Some workers had supplemented the little knowledge given by parents with information provided by other relatives, a sibling's social worker, or the child's guardian. Six workers had relied entirely upon information recorded in the files from earlier work with the family, as the parent(s)' whereabouts were unknown or they refused all contact with the department.

Ensuring that the information that went on children's files was accurate was also of concern. Some birth parents had given inconsistent or untruthful responses and, in a few cases, social workers had to proceed very slowly due to parental mental ill health, as in the following example.

All those interviews were conducted with [mother] through a French interpreter. It had to be taken very slowly and over a period of time because of her psychiatric illness, but we got there in the end, and we had quite a full and comprehensive picture that mum's been able to [give] about those issues.

Three workers reported parental reluctance to discuss their backgrounds because of traumatic experiences in other countries.

Only a few social workers (3) described the experience of talking to co-operative parents and where the worker herself was confident about discussing cultural issues. One social worker said:

. . . the parents are very open in talking to me. For example, they told me the village, etc, where they came from and stuff like that, so it was, you know, fairly easy. And that was simply because (. . .) of the

relationship that I've been able to build up with the parents.
Otherwise, I think that might have been quite difficult.

Most social workers recognised that there were gaps in the information they had gathered and hoped to fill them once the court hearings had been completed. Only one worker thought there had been insufficient efforts to gain information on the birth father and two white workers thought that a minority ethnic social worker might have been more successful.

Birth parents' wishes

Although most parents were not supporting the adoption plan, 28 had made their wishes known about what kind of family they would like for their child. A religious match was important for 13 parents, and most of these were requests for the child to be raised as a Muslim, as in the following example.

> *I know that she [mother] did mention she would like him to be raised with a Pakistani family and I did have to say, 'Well, there might not be a Pakistani family – would you be OK with that?' and she said, 'Yes, as long as they're Muslim and they're . . . and they take good care of him'. Those were the main things, she sort of went through it – going to take good care of him and yes, she was fine.*

These birth parents had also made specific requests about continuing cultural practices such as circumcision, diet, dress, and attending classes at the mosque. Two white English mothers did not want their white/ Pakistani children raised as Muslims and had requested a white adoptive family. A few birth parents (8) had told the social worker that what they wanted most for their child was to have a good start in life, to do well in school, and for adopters to teach "right and wrong". Birth parents wanted their child to be placed in a caring, loving, and supportive family and to have information about the birth parents and extended family.

Most of the social workers thought that the birth parents' wishes should be complied with to some degree, but this depended on the availability of adopters and whether the wishes of the birth parent were compatible with the best interests of the child.

I think it's important to listen and to try and discuss it and look at all different angles. I don't think that you can always do what the birth parents want.

Although only one birth parent had asked to be involved in choosing the adopters, many other social workers hoped that more parents would eventually be involved. Only two social workers mentioned finding out what the wishes of extended family members were in relation to matching. One planned to visit the maternal grandparents and the other had consulted grandparents who lived outside the UK.

Contact plans after adoption

Social workers stated that they were planning for most children to have letterbox contact with their mothers and for slightly fewer children to have contact with their fathers. Nearly a quarter of children had complex contact plans involving mothers, fathers and extended family members. In contrast, five children were not expected to have contact with their parents and two children had no contact planned with anyone.

Table 11.4
Social work plans for children and family contact after adoption (n=50)

	Mother	Father	Siblings	Extended family
Face-to-face	2	1	15	2
Indirect contact	37	30	11	15

Social workers' matching criteria

Social workers were asked to describe what the child needed from an adoptive placement. At the top of most of their "wishlists" was the child's need for a loving, warm, stable family and adopters who were responsive to the needs of the child, as described below.

Well, she'll need what any other child of her age will need – security, stability, a good standard of care, love, affection, attention . . . She'll need the adopters to be open and honest about the fact that she's adopted, and to be able to explain to her when she's old enough to understand why she's been placed for adoption.

Just over a quarter (28%) of social workers wanted adopters who would be able to help the child with grief and loss or attachment and behavioural difficulties, while also supporting contact plans and meeting health or educational needs.

Some were looking for specific characteristics in the prospective adopters, for example: adopters who had adopted before; or had older children; adopters who had time; or who had animals; or with an extended family nearby; who had a slightly chaotic household; adopters who would enable the child to grow up as a responsible member of society; who would take the child to the birth mother's country of birth; who had contact with other cultures; who were not judgemental about drug-using parents; or a couple who were committed to each other. Many workers wanted two parents who already had children, as described by one social worker.

I think a family where there'd be some older children in the family would be quite good for [child] because she seems to be very used to interacting with people now, especially since she's been in foster care. She's had two older foster siblings and I think she's got quite used to that attention now, so it'd be nice if she did have a good family where there's at least one older child whom she could play with.

Over half did not mention the structure of the adopter's family or thought that any type would be acceptable. These workers emphasised the child's needs more than the family structure, but the language used was still predominantly of "families" and "couples", as in the example below.

I don't really care whether it's a couple or a family, I just want somebody who would be able to meet [child's] needs as a little baby growing up, cultural needs as well. And I think . . . an ideal couple obviously would be similar cultural backgrounds to the parents.

Other social workers (44%) were explicit about their ideal adoptive family – usually a couple who already had children. A few went on to explain why a couple would be "ideal" or best suited to parenting the child, and the reasons given did not always link clearly to the child's needs.

Ideal parents would be, I would say, young, a young professional couple, in a big house and lots of money. . . . I think it'd be nice for him because I've seen him with older children . . . if he had an older brother or sister . . . that he has adoptive parents who will definitely promote sibling contact . . .

A young couple with energy and enthusiasm. A couple, rather than a man or woman, because he's going to be hard to look after and I think it will place a lot of pressure if it was a single carer. I would consider it, but it would be a second best. He is quite an active child and quite possibly his future will involve doing lots of activities like football, so if it was a single carer it would be someone who could be doing that . . .

In the interview, social workers were asked if they would consider a single person or lesbians/gay men as adopters. A greater number (82%) said they would consider single women and lesbian carers than male gay carers (64%). However, it is difficult to know if they would follow this through in practice. A few workers explained why they would not consider a single male or male couple.

A single male? . . . It's just that he's male and [child] is used to having females as his carers and also he's very attached to his mother. If we deprive him of the mother in his life and then there is not any female that he can form an attachment with, and having been raised by a female household all these years, I think that would really have a major impact on him.

Only one person admitted to holding views that are more conservative.

Well, I'm quite conservative in my thinking. I mean there are matches that are approved all the time – same-sex couples. I'd say I'd consider a lesbian couple but not a same-sex gay male. No, I wouldn't consider that. I would obviously have to discuss with the family finder and see what panel says, but personally . . . I'm quite conservative on that.

When talking about the prospective adoptive families and the child's needs, none of the social workers referred to the Assessment Framework or any other conceptual models for thinking about the placement needs of a child.

Cultural, ethnic and religious matching

Most social workers (96%) thought that children's needs were best met in an ethnically matched placement, as expressed in the following interview extracts.

> *I'd want an Asian family... where both partners are Asian and ideally from Pakistan and ideally Muslim, because that would have been what he was raised as.*

> *Two parents, one white, one Asian ... [who] will be understanding and sympathetic to his early experiences ... [who] will bring him up within the Islamic faith, and ... [who] can just offer him a high level of parenting.*

In cases where an exact match was wanted, many children were placed with foster carers whom the social worker viewed as either matched (11) or providing some match (3) such as in the case of a Somali Arabic-speaking child who was placed with Moroccan Arabic-speaking foster carers. Exact matches on the child's ethnicity were being sought for all the children (9) whose first language was not English and this suggests that non-English speakers might make exact matching on ethnicity more likely.

Some children had less common ethnicities such as white/Cuban or white/Japanese, or ethnicity was not mentioned by the social worker. Interestingly, none of these children were in fully matched foster placements and eight out of 11 were placed with white foster carers. This raises the question of whether being placed with white foster carers, or in a placement with no ethnic match, increases the likelihood that little or no importance will be attached to finding an ethnically matched or similar adoptive placement. In one case, the social worker stated that she did not know enough about the child's parentage to know whether the Asian foster carers shared the child's ethnicity.

Although many social workers wanted an exact match on ethnicity, they recognised that this might not be possible. About three-quarters of the workers, when asked how close the ethnic match needed to be, thought "some match" was acceptable. The workers cited the lack of available adopters, especially for mixed ethnicity children, the need to reduce delay, and the difficulties of finding adopters willing to support children whose ethnicity was uncertain.

We may never find out what his ethnicity is and we're going to need a placement that's going to be able to . . . handle that uncertainty themselves but also to be able to try and promote, as far as possible, [child's] identity, in a way that doesn't end up making him feel left out or different . . .

There was no statistical relationship between the social worker's own ethnicity and attention to the ethnicity of future adopters. Although workers were aware they might not find an exact ethnic match, most were hopeful of finding adopters who would be sensitive to the child's culture.

She's really going to need somebody who's going to have a cultural understanding to try and help her with her culture and ethnicity. Language – less of an issue, I think. I don't think we could stick out for somebody who's going to be able to teach her her language, but I think if we can just get her having positive identity about being Indian, we've achieved something . . . I'm realistic and I know that finding adopters who are dual heritage, it is just going to be very difficult, but we haven't got any geographical limitations to that so it might be achievable. Failing that, we'd need to have somebody who'd have links with that community, the usual sort of going down the "hit list" really, in terms of the racial issues . . .

In the event of no suitable minority ethnic adopters, 18 social workers stated that white adopters might be considered, especially if they had contact with people from other cultures and an understanding of racism. Another explained that a number of possibilities would be considered.

Ideally, where's there's one parent who is African and one who is white British and then move down the "hit list" to what is closest to that. If that's not achievable, then you have to move down in terms of Afro-Caribbean/white British, and then white British with a lot of interest in the African community or vice versa, and then single carers who were African or white British.

Some workers were also concerned about the kind of neighbourhood where the child would live. Most wanted a multicultural area where there was a population of ethnicity similar to that of the child, or emphasised an area similar to where the child had already lived, as explained below.

Ideally, it would be [a] Bengali Sylheti-speaking neighbourhood, or at least a mixed neighbourhood where there was a community of Bengali Sylheti speakers, where there was a mosque.

Others were less concerned about the diversity of a neighbourhood and wanted an area with good opportunities and low crime. A few workers mentioned the importance of an ethnically mixed local school. Ten per cent were unconcerned about the neighbourhood and did not consider it an important factor:

. . . to be honest, I don't think it really matters at all where he lives.

Social workers' views on "ethnic matching" were complex, sometimes contradictory and sometimes pragmatic. When asked what children needed from their adoptive families, half of the workers discussed the child's need to have adopters of the same ethnicity. When asked what qualities and characteristics they were looking for in an adoptive family, 68 per cent were concerned about the ethnicity of the prospective adopters. However, when asked directly about matching, only 18 per cent stated they wanted an exact match and 78 per cent thought some match was sought. Two workers were not looking for any kind of match, as in the following example.

Well, I suppose she might want some information about . . . Iraqi life but no particular needs [around her culture, religion, ethnicity, identity] really.

Twenty-two per cent of social workers thought that religion was a very important element in matching. For example, one social worker commented:

> *. . . definitely we would be placing this boy in a Muslim family because . . . it's going to be a very important piece of his life, especially when he has sibling contact . . . I always look at the future when this boy reads his file. He may come back and read his file. 'Oh, I'm from a Muslim family, why wasn't I placed with a Muslim? Why was I placed with a Christian family?' However, to read the Koran, [child] is actually going to another service to learn to speak Arabic . . . so as adoptive parents we will be expecting that definitely.*

Other considerations in matching

Social workers were also asked about the importance of the adopters' financial stability. Surprisingly, this was still an important consideration for half of the workers. Only 14 per cent said it was of no importance. Four workers also emphasised that they would prefer adopters who closely physically resembled the birth parents, as in the following interview extract:

> *Well, what I do, I really look at the birth parents and I usually look at their ethnicity. That's how I've always done it and to match that way, so even in terms of, like, ages, the way they look, hair, colour, I'll try and match . . . If I see a couple or an individual adoptive carer, then I'll try and match them with the birth parents as much as possible.*

The most important criteria for matching

During the interview, social workers discussed many factors which they considered important in matching. We asked workers which of these mattered the most and to name their most important criteria (see Table 11.5).

Table 11.5
Social workers' most essential criteria when searching for adopters

Criteria	*Percentage of social workers (n = 49)* %
Ethnicity, culture and promoting positive identity	48%
Warmth, love, commitment and putting child's needs first	14%
Religious match	6%
Able to meet health needs	6%
Stability and being able to maintain routines	6%
Able to support contact	6%
Able to work with child's attachment difficulties	4%
Able to support educational needs	4%
Sibling group placement	2%
Able to support and engage in life story work	2%
Parenting experience	2%
Understanding of the issues and impact of racism	2%
Able to be positive about the birth family	2%

Family-finding process

A few prospective adoptive families had been identified before the panel met. Plans were that two children would be placed with the families who had adopted their siblings, and one was to be placed with distant relatives. In addition, three children had families tentatively identified from the in-house pool of prospective adopters.

It was surprising to find that eight social workers had no knowledge at all of the family-finding process. One social worker stated:

No, to be honest I couldn't really comment that much on the process that they [family-finding team] do because I don't know. I don't have anything to do with that.

Most of the children's social workers knew little about the process and thought that many avenues would be tried in order to find an appropriate family (see Table 11.6).

Table 11.6
Children's social workers' expectations of the extent of family-finding activity

Family-finding activity	*Expected number of children who would benefit*
Family-finding publications	18
Local consortium search	16
Adoption register entry	11
Only in-house and local resources	10
Other adverts – local press, Adoption UK	6
"Private" agencies	2
Use of minority ethnic press	1

The use of voluntary adoption agencies were not mentioned as a resource by any of the social workers, although two referred to "private agencies", which we assume to mean voluntary agencies. Eighteen social workers did not know if there were any financial constraints on family finding but most workers expected that efforts would be tried sequentially, as described by the social worker in the extract below:

> *They'll [the family finder] take it to a meeting and see if we've got anybody in-house. They'll look at it at their team meeting and, if they have, they then present you with usually two choices. If they haven't got anybody in-house, I would ask them to look at the consortium . . . and if there's nobody suitable there, then they'd go nationwide, I guess.*

There were only seven children (14%) whose social workers thought that multiple sources would be used to find a family. These children were all infants, which suggests that workers might place more emphasis on moving younger children (under 3 years) quickly into an adoptive family rather than older children. This might also reflect pessimistic views of the chances of finding adopters for older children.

Interestingly, there were different approaches to the use of promotion in family finding. Some workers did not think promotion would be necessary for their child, as they believed they would be easy to place, whilst other social workers expected to use promotion proactively, as described below:

> *In terms of financial issues generally, [local authority] are quite good. With previous children that I've had, we've advertised in Disability Now, in Diva, in The Guardian, in the Nursing Times . . .*

Another worker, who did not know about the family-finding process, disliked the idea of promotions and when asked about *Be My Parent* responded:

> Social worker: *I think it's quite cruel – Be My Parent.*

> Interviewer: *It's quite cruel?*

> Social worker: *Yes. It's like you're looking and you take a pick . . . But then, I know a few children who have been successfully adopted through there. Actually, you turn pages of the magazine and you pick and choose. So hopefully, it wouldn't have to get to that stage.*

Fifteen social workers identified a range of local authority constraints in finding a family for the child. These included not enough time dedicated to family finding, pressure to accept in-house families, and financial limitations around the use of advertising.

Ease of finding a "matched" adoptive placement

Social workers were asked how easy they thought it would be to find a family for the child. The majority of social workers (45%) thought there would be some difficulties, or it would be very or extremely difficult (16%). Just over a third (36%) thought that finding the right adoptive family would be easy. When asked why they thought it would be difficult to find a family, most gave reasons that included the child's age, ethnicity and history, as in the extract below:

> *Her age, the fact that she's dual heritage, and I think when adoptive families read the information that they're given, they will see that she's had significant changes . . . from birth going into foster care, then returning to her mum at six months old, and then being removed again at three, so they're crucial stages in her development and attachment and bonding, and I think most adopters would worry about that.*

Two social workers, who thought it would be "extremely difficult" to find a matched placement, referred to the child's ethnicity, with one also mentioning the need to find an insightful family:

> *Well, because it's very hard to find matching carers for children of that ethnicity.* [Somali Muslim child]

> *We're asking for very specific adopters, aren't we? We're asking either for African-Caribbean adopters or mixed dual heritage adopters . . . There are all the other factors that [child] needs as well. It has to be, because even if you get someone of the same background, cultural background, if they haven't got the right insights, they're not going to be right . . .*

We expected the child's age to be mentioned as a reason for older children being "hard to place", but were surprised when it was mentioned as a factor for children as young as one year old.

Waiting and changes of plan

Social workers were asked how long they were prepared to wait for their ideal adoptive family before altering the plan. Most (66%) thought changes would be made six months later if adopters had not been found; 20 per cent thought changes would be made 7–12 months later; five per cent would wait more than a year; and nine per cent did not know how long they would wait. If a suitable adoptive family could not be found,

Table 11.7
Social workers' reasons for why finding adopters might prove difficult

Reason	Number of social workers
Ethnicity	20
Child's age	10
Culture	6
Religion and language	4
Emotional and behavioural difficulties	4
Complex contact plans	4
Geographical location	4
Physical impairment	2
Sibling placement	2

most said they would widen the possible pool of adopters by including prospective adopters of another minority ethnicity (49%), and/or considering white prospective adopters (43%), and that this might involve increased promotion or using adopters from another local authority. A few social workers (11%) said that plans would be likely to change to long-term foster care, and three workers had not considered what course of action might be taken.

Some of the social workers who said they might consider broadening the criteria were not confident about how they would assess whether the prospective adopters could meet the child's needs, as in the following interview extract:

Actually, I don't know [which other backgrounds]. I don't know which would be most suitable, because then what I would look at would be, is the family able to provide . . . if they do not have the knowledge, are they willing to acquire knowledge of [child's] cultural background?

The children who might be the focus of such a decision (to place with white adopters) were aged between four months and 11 years and all but one was of mixed parentage and English-speaking. Three were Muslim, including one Bangladeshi child whose first language was Sylheti and about whom the social worker said:

> *For instance, [I would consider] placing [child] with a white family who have significant connections with the Muslim community. For instance, they could have relatives who are married to somebody of the Islamic faith. Or they live in a community where they have access to resources that can meet his religious needs.*

Adoption support

Adoptive families

Despite all we know about the importance of support services for adoptive parents, no support was planned for the adoptive parents of three children. Two social workers explained their thinking, with one stating that support could not be addressed before the adopters were identified, and the other insisting that the adopters would require minimal support as this was a relinquished baby, as in the extract below.

> *They would get support from their worker. I wouldn't envisage them needing a whole host of support . . . His experiences aren't going to be abuse or neglect. He's obviously going to have to struggle to understand why his mum didn't want him, but compared to other children, I think we're going to have quite an ideal baby really.*

Seventy-four per cent of workers referred to non-specific adoption support services. This suggests that, at this stage, they had given little thought to the support adopters might need in relation to the child. Some saw this as the job of the permanency team or the adoption support team, but others had little adoption practice experience and were uncertain about the services available, as in the extract below:

> *They [the adopters] do have support, I don't know exactly, off my head . . . I think for [a] certain period the adoptive parents have a sort of supervising social worker. There are other [supports] . . . Adopters' parents group . . . The financial side to it, I'm not quite*

keen on, but ... you're really taking on a parenting role, so a part of the assessment would have been, can these people financially make do? But yes, there are some after adoption, post-adoption services offered. I'm sure there's drop-in centres.

A few (10) social workers were able to identify support services that they hoped would be provided, such as an adoption allowance, although several of them were unclear about the criteria for eligibility. Support groups were suggested by six of the more experienced workers as a way of providing adopters with specific help, for example, in parenting a disabled child or dealing with cultural issues:

I would hope that there is some sort of support. Certainly, adopters do lean on other people who they know have adopted children. That can prove to be a very good support ... quite useful for the early stages in what can be potential difficulties and sort of aspects of problem-solving and how to get around that, really.

Seven social workers thought that adoption support would include help with contact arrangements, including help in writing letters to the birth family, payments to facilitate direct contact, and support in handling any conflict. Responding to the evolving nature of contact and, when the child grows up, making contact with birth family overseas, were also mentioned, as in the extract below.

And I'd like adopters to have support in an ongoing way, because the contact may change over time and he may, as he gets older, decide he wants more contact with his birth family.

Providing post-adoption support to adoptive families specifically around issues of ethnicity, culture, language or religion had already been planned for four of the 50 children. This was not restricted to non-matched placements, as one social worker said:

That's what I'm saying, support in case they are not from that background and sometimes even if they are of the same background.

183

None of the social workers mentioned support to adoptive families around challenging racism. Four workers cited other forms of adoption support, including talking with the adopters about the child's life history and helping adopters to respond to children's questions about their past:

> *I think in terms of the adoptive family, it's really important that they have, again, support in terms of full knowledge and understanding, as far as it's available, of [child's] background and her needs – and even though they've been assessed, etc, looking at her specific needs, trying to put in any support around those issues . . .*

Birth parents

No support was planned for 12 per cent of birth parents, but half of the children's social workers hoped that birth parents would have the opportunity for counselling in the future. There was also some recognition that siblings and extended family members might benefit from support too, as in the following extracts from interviews:

> *Well, definitely for the parents, they'd need some form of counselling. And I think, possibly not straight away. I think it's something that might hit them later on . . .*

> *[Father] would be referred to the [regional adoption support agency]. We do that automatically in [local authority] when it's come through panel, so that the person's put in contact with them . . . they would also be doing support, for instance, if we asked them for [child's] brother, also for mum and any paternal relatives . . .*

Counselling was viewed as needed in order to address a number of issues, such as a birth mother's own adoption, children's non-accidental injuries, and the loss of the child through adoption, as this social worker explained.

> *I think the main thing for them would be counselling, to kind of work through 1) why has this child been injured in this way? [. . .] And that 2) counselling around having their child removed from their care and then placed with another family . . . and all of the issues that that brings up and raises for them.*

Social workers also thought that counselling might help the birth parents to understand the adoption process and the process of letterbox contact. Specific help with contact was to be offered to eight birth parents to help them to engage, to offer support around setting up the letterbox contact arrangement, and to help with writing letters, as this social worker said:

> ... helping them write, letterbox contact and what's appropriate what's not appropriate to write, so that can continue smoothly. I think one of the big flaws in that is parents don't get support in that, they write the wrong thing, the adopters panic and then it all falls apart.

A few workers (5) hoped that birth parents would be offered the chance to attend a support group or be given advice about regional or independent support services. However, some thought it very unlikely that birth parents would make use of adoption support services:

> Yes, we'll offer the birth parents post-adoption support but, as I say, they won't take it up.

Adopted children

Social workers were asked what kind of support they would like to see offered to the child post placement. As with adoptive parents and birth parents, not all children were seen as requiring adoption support services. Counselling as the child grew older, and sometimes throughout life, was often emphasised. Some workers identified areas that this might focus on, such as having been adopted, the questions a child might have as he or she grew up, the experience of sexual abuse, the adoptive family, reading one's file, and tracing the birth family. One social worker said:

> I would like him to have access throughout his life, and in an appropriate way, to counselling. I don't think that would come off, but I'd like there to be some post-adoption support for him that he can tap into whenever he needs to, whenever he wants to, to be able to work through issues of: Why was I adopted? What happened to me? Why aren't I with my mum and dad?

Two workers had plans in place to offer the child help with contact, including keeping in touch with a foster carer and making contact with birth family overseas. Only one social worker mentioned the availability of support groups and help for children around their language, ethnicity, religion or the experience of racism.

Support from other agencies

Social workers were asked whether they envisaged other agencies providing support to birth parents, children, or adoptive parents post placement. There was little identified need for support. It was hoped that 11 birth parents would continue to receive or begin to attend drug or alcohol services and have help with their mental health problems. A few social workers also mentioned other services such as probation and the need for independent support for birth parents once the adoption decision was made.

Community child health services and hospital outpatients services were needed for 12 children and additional educational services were needed for four children with learning difficulties. It was hoped that CAMHS would continue to be involved with eight children.

Social workers' views about attending the adoption panel

Most social workers had experience of going to panel, but for six of them, the presentation of the child's case was to be their first time. The majority (64%) had anxieties about going to panel and over a third were worried about their own performance because there had been so many recent legal and procedural changes. A few (4) were anxious because of previous experiences at panel or about how a particular panel member might respond, and three were worried about the outcome. Most (90%) thought that the panel members would ask questions about a range of issues including finding a match, whether kinship options had been fully explored, contact plans, arrangements for siblings, information about the birth family, the quality of the child's assessment, and whether the child had been prepared. Thirty-six per cent gave other responses, ranging from not knowing what issues might be raised through to anticipating questions about health, attachment, and identity issues, such as in the following example.

Yes, [child's] health ... They'll probably want him testing for HIV, hepatitis. They just generally randomly test any child that's been born drug dependent and I don't necessarily agree with that. Attachment, they'll pick up on attachment: how ... because he was moved at a significant time in his life ... how that's going to affect his future ability to attach. They'll probably ... label him as having uncertain development.

About three-quarters of the social workers were not aware of any particular attitudes or opinions that panel members might hold regarding minority ethnic children but almost half (44%) thought that the panel would be strongly in favour of "same-race" placements. Most social workers were confident that the panel would make an adoption recommendation, but four per cent thought there was only a 50/50 chance of that happening.

Following the interviews with the social workers, the 50 children were tracked by monthly telephone calls until July 2007, the outcomes of which are discussed in the next chapter.

Summary

- The interview sample comprised 49 social workers working with 50 minority ethnic children who were to be considered for an adoption recommendation between November 2005 and December 2006.
- The majority (74%) of the children were of mixed ethnicity, 22 per cent were Asian and four per cent black. The social workers' ethnicities were 51 per cent white, 13 per cent black, seven per cent Asian and eight per cent were of mixed ethnicity.
- Social workers said they knew the children well, but 38 per cent had first met the child within the last four weeks and only 16 per cent of the children had had the same social worker throughout their involvement with Children's Services.
- Over half (54%) of the children's social workers thought that white children were more likely to be placed for adoption and that they would be better matched than minority ethnic children. Social workers identified mixed ethnicity children as particularly problematic to place

and a few were pessimistic about finding an adoptive placement for the child.

- Social workers thought that adoption procedures and regulations deterred minority ethnic adopters, and that Eurocentric assessments and current recruitment techniques reflected a lack of sensitivity to "race" and ethnicity issues.

- There were gaps in information about the birth parents, often because the parents were unco-operative or they had not been asked, as reunification was still a possibility. Some social workers assumed (incorrectly) that the parents shared the same culture as each other.

- Twenty-eight birth parents had made specific requests about the kind of adoptive family they wanted for their child and 13 of these requests were about matching on the basis of the child's religion.

- Eight workers knew nothing about the family-finding process and others were vague. Most social workers (96%) thought that children's needs were best met in an ethnically matched placement. However, recognising that this might not be possible, 78 per cent were seeking a placement where a part of the child's ethnicity was matched.

- Children who were living in an ethnically matched foster placement and whose first language was not English were being sought an exactly matched placement.

- There were only seven children (all infants) whose social workers thought that many different sources and agencies would be considered to find an adoptive family.

- The social workers' top criteria when searching for adopters were ethnicity, culture and promoting positive identity (mentioned by 48%) and warmth, love, commitment and putting a child's needs first (mentioned by 14%).

- Most social workers (66%) thought the plan should change within six months if adopters had not been found. If they could not get a match, 49 per cent said they would consider prospective adopters of another minority ethnicity and 43 per cent would consider white adopters.

- Not all adoptive parents, birth parents or children were seen as needing access to adoption support services.

12 Follow-up telephone interviews with children's social workers

We planned to follow up the 49 face-to-face interviews with monthly telephone calls to find out how plans were taking shape. Calls continued until the child was placed or until the end of data collection in January 2007. One final telephone call was made between June and August 2007 to check on whether adoptive families had been found and where the children had been placed.

The first follow-up telephone call

Three weeks after the panel had met, the first round of telephone calls were made to children's social workers. The intention was to ask workers about their experiences at the adoption panel and if family finding had begun. However, the panel had never seen 11 (22%) children's papers, and most of these children (73%) were from the Northern authority. It was surprising that so many plans had changed so quickly, as interviews had taken place very close to the date of the panel booking.

Changes of plan before the panel met

Plans had changed and subsequent panel bookings had been cancelled because:

- Four children had twin-track plans (reunification or adoption) and one child a triple plan (reunification or kinship care or adoption). All five children returned home but one child quickly became looked after again following abuse, but the plan for adoption was not followed up.
- Three children were placed with kin (one on the direction of the court).
- Two children's panel bookings were cancelled because social workers decided to undertake more assessments of kin. At the final follow-up in 2007, these cases had still not gone to panel.
- One child's panel booking was cancelled, as the local authority legal department insisted that twin-tracking was illegal.

Cases that reached the adoption panel

Thirty-nine children's cases reached the panel (one black, eight Asian and 30 mixed ethnicity children), and 36 of these had an adoption recommendation made by the panel. Decisions were deferred in three cases, as the panel requested more information about the child's health, the birth parents, and family history.

The researcher asked social workers about their experiences of attending the panel meeting. Most were pleased with the way the meeting had gone and were happy with the way they had presented the case, with a quarter reporting that panel members had been complimentary about the quality of their work. Just one worker had been upset by the experience.

Surprisingly, only 54 per cent of social workers said that panel members had enquired about the child's culture, ethnicity, religion or language. Panel members had asked specific questions and wanted more detail about the children's fathers, particularly when paternity was disputed or ethnicity was unknown. A few social workers were uncomfortable with the emphasis by some panel members on the uncertainty of the child's ethnicity, as they thought it created additional difficulties in family finding. There had also been discussion at the panel about what kind of family should be sought in cases where white birth mothers had expressed a wish that their mixed ethnicity child should be placed with white families.

Changes of plan after the panel had met and further assessments of kin

The first follow-up telephone call also revealed that, after the panel had recommended adoption, the adoption plan had been put "on hold" for three children. Courts had ordered more kin assessments in respect of two children and refused to allow any promotion until these assessments were complete. Another child had more kin assessed for their suitability to care, because of a social work decision.

Social workers did voice their irritation at being directed by courts to carry out these additional kin assessments, when they were sure that the relatives would prove to be unsuitable. For example, in one case the relatives believed, as did the mother, that the child was controlled by

Djinn (demons). This led to the relatives withdrawing from the court-ordered assessment, and the social worker commented:

Assessing family members has caused a lot of delay and we have to consider them, although in my report to the court for August 2007, I am recommending that we do not continue to do so.

However, there were some examples of lengthy delays with positive outcomes. In one case, a social worker travelled to Jamaica to assess the child's birth father and his support network. The father was not named on the birth certificate and DNA tests had to be completed. This took many months. All the social work, guardian and other reports indicated that the father would be a good carer and in the view of the court, this was an excellent piece of social work practice. It had a positive outcome with the child being placed with his father.

Finding adoptive families

One month after the panel had met, new families had already been found for nine of the children. Four children were moving into adoptive families who had already adopted one of their siblings; another four adoptive families had been found in-house; and one child had been placed with kin. In this latter case, the social worker had recommended a Residence Order, but was over-ruled by the judge who insisted on making an Adoption Order. Interestingly, in the birth family's view, this was a kinship placement but in the eyes of the court it was a "stranger" adoption because the relationship of the carer to the child was through marriage and very distant.

Families for 27 children still needed to be found and social workers were asked if they were actively seeking families and how it was progressing. Most children's social workers stated that nothing was happening as, until a worker from the family-finding team had been allocated, activity could not begin. However, children's social workers expected the child to be allocated to someone in the team within the following four weeks.

In three cases, court-related issues were preventing family finding. In one case, a Care Order had not been obtained and, as the birth mother was missing, the court had delayed its decision. Kin assessments were not complete in another, and in the third, the social worker stated that she needed court approval before being allowed to promote the child.

Family finding was taking place for ten children but none had been promoted as all efforts had been focused on looking in-house and through the consortiums. There were plans to use an Adoption Exchange Day focusing on minority ethnic children and families to family-find for one child.

The children's social workers were asked if they had any concerns about the likelihood of finding an adoptive family. Four workers thought that uncertainty about the child's development or court delays would make family finding more difficult for the child. One child's social worker disliked giving all the control to the family-finding team. Others voiced their confusion and frustration about meeting the needs of mixed ethnicity children:

How do you prioritise different dual heritage couples, compared with the need for adopters to have a good understanding and acceptance of long-term developmental issues?

Who does reply to adverts? There is a lack of adopters from the same ethnic backgrounds – those that reply are from different ethnic backgrounds.

Subsequent follow-up calls

Monthly telephone calls continued to be made throughout 2006 and 2007 until the child was placed or data collection ceased. The monthly calls, although time-consuming, were an important way of tracking each child's progress. It was through these calls that we learnt about changes of plan or change of social worker and about delays due to court processes or staff sickness. The final call in July/August 2007 was the most difficult to complete. Many social workers had changed or had moved offices, and although we had allowed a month to make the fifty calls, it actually took nearly three months to trace all the children and their current workers.

Only 29 (59%) of the 49 social workers who had been originally interviewed were still the current social worker. Many children (n = 21) had had two different social workers and some had more (range 1–4) from the date of the panel adoption recommendation. During the final telephone call to children's social workers, we asked how many prospective adopters had shown interest in the child. Many (20) social workers did not know, as they were either a new worker or said that the information was held by the family-finding team. Where social workers could provide information, 40 per cent of children had had one or two potential prospective adopters, and 30 per cent had four or more. Twelve potential adopters had been interested in a child with FASD, but none had been suitable and the social worker commented that they had 'not been able to meet the child's complex needs'.

Table 12.1 below outlines the children's placements at the time of the final follow-up call. Adoption was no longer the plan for 17 (34%) of the 50 children.

Adoptive placements

Just 13 of the children had been placed for adoption. Two had been placed through promotions in *Be My Parent* or *Children Who Wait*. A family had been found for another child after a successful promotion in the Black press, and yet another child was placed after the Adoption Register identified a potential match. Just as in the other samples, mixed ethnicity children had been placed quicker (average 30 weeks) than Asian children

Table 12.1
Placements at July/August 2007

	Black *(n = 2)*	*Asian* *(n = 11)*	*Mixed* *(n = 37)*
Stranger adoption	–	3	10
"Waiting" for a permanent placement	–	3	16
Kinship placement	1	4	6
Long-term local authority foster care	–	–	3
Reunified	1	1	1

(average 48 weeks). Neither of the two black children had been placed with an adoptive family. There were no statistical differences between the authorities on whether the child had been placed for adoption, nor did the ethnicity of the child's social worker or their experience in adoption practice make a significant difference.

Most children had been placed with heterosexual couples and just one Asian child had been placed with a single carer (Asian). Seven children had been placed where there were other children (range 1–4 other children) and five had been placed with some or all of their siblings. Although these children had been placed, five workers described delays in family finding mainly due to changes of social worker or the worker having extended sick leave. In one case, where a child had ten siblings in different adoptive placements, the prospect of twice-yearly sibling contact was thought to have deterred some of the prospective adopters.

Ethnicity and matching

Five mixed ethnicity children had been placed in mono-ethnic families[45] (three in families where both adults were white and two in Asian families). All except one family were said by the social worker to be living in a culturally diverse area. Five other mixed ethnicity children were living in adoptive families, where the parents were in an ethnically mixed relationship and/or where one partner was of mixed ethnicity themselves. All the Asian children had been placed in Asian Muslim adoptive families.

Support

Social workers again commented that, although support had been offered to birth parents, most declined. Only three birth mothers were currently receiving services. Fewer than three-quarters of adopters had been offered adoption support services such as attending support groups. Most were still receiving monthly social work visits, as Adoption Orders had not been made.

---

[45] We have used the term mono-ethnic but recognise that this is problematic because all human beings have multiple heritages.

Children still waiting (n = 19)

There were 19 children still waiting for an adoptive placement. Six of them looked likely to be placed, as there was a family "waiting in the wings". However, social workers were pessimistic about the chances of finding adopters for 13 waiting children. It was therefore surprising to find that only ten of the 50 children had been promoted. One child had appeared in the BBC *Families Wanted* series and was still waiting and another six children were still waiting after promotions in family-finding publications.

New health information had emerged for three children and social workers thought this would "put adopters off". It was difficult to know how much effort had been put into recruiting adopters for children with disabilities or those who had genetic risks, as workers were so pessimistic about the children's chances. It was also unclear how far the net had been widened to consider adopters of other ethnicities, as in the example below:

> *Primarily [child] has quite unspecified needs in terms of her physical development. The other issue is the Polish side of the child's heritage – adopters have pulled out saying they could not meet her needs in terms of the Polish side of her needs. We were going for white/Asian adopters initially, a Muslim family. We have had to go for non-practising Muslims, as we could search for ever (. . .) her ethnicity has put people off, even before we have explored her developmental concerns*

Multiple assessments also had an impact on the chances of adoption for some of the children who were still waiting. Three children's parents had had multiple assessments to see if they were able to parent the child. While the assessments were taking place, no other family-finding activity had taken place, as in the example below.

Illustrative example

The birth mother, Stacey, was a young white English woman, herself looked after with problems of drug misuse and a history of relationships with violent men. Her son, Jay, was put on the Child Protection Register at birth (2003) and Stacey asked that he be accommodated at four months old. The infant was placed in short-term foster care and then returned to his mother and current partner for a period of assessment during which concerns remained about poor parenting and domestic violence. Stacey asked for Jay to be adopted and a Care Order was made in 2004.

However, Stacey had had two further negative assessments, and with regard to the father, one assessment stopped when he went missing; during the second, he was sent to prison; and in the third he failed to reveal a new partner and child. There was even more delay when assessments of paternal relatives were undertaken in the USA. In 2007, the social work plan was still a twin-track plan for reunification and adoption. The social worker stated that Jay would be difficult to place for adoption, and the birth father with his new partner was currently undergoing a fourth assessment. In the meantime, Jay had had three short-term white foster carers. The new social worker commented:

Very disappointing that the child has been in care for such a long time . . . shame permanency has not been secured earlier for this child.

Lack of legal orders also caused delay, as this prevented children from being promoted. Other children were still waiting because of the wish to place them in a "same-race" placement. One child was in short-term foster care after the adopters of the child's siblings had been turned down because the child was thought to be of a different ethnicity to her siblings. In this case, the birth mother had requested a Muslim adoptive placement (although she was white and had no religion), and in the interview, the social worker stated:

We decided that ethnicity and language and the religious needs of the child would not be met if she was placed with her half-sibling.

Minority ethnicity was often seen as a problem, particularly that of mixed ethnicity children. Promotions, where they had occurred, had been sequential and sometimes this approach was justified in terms of the child's ethnicity:

Because of his dual heritage we only looked at one [adopter] at a time.

His background is dual heritage – Asian Pakistani/white British. Culturally the child's background is very white British. It's really disappointing. We have trawled nationally – not a huge response. When people hear the implications of drug use in pregnancy, they lose interest. Hopefully, we'll find a family next week on the Asian Network broadcast.

Children whose plan had changed away from adoption

Reunification (n = 4)

Four children had been returned to their mother's care. One Asian child was returned after the mother decided to tell her own family about the child's birth and, instead of the rejection she feared, they accepted her and the baby. Two children were returned after the mother's mental health improved significantly and another child went back to live with his mother in Japan, as the English courts had no jurisdiction over a child with Japanese citizenship.

Kinship care (n=11)

Eleven children were living with relatives: two with an Adoption Order, three with Special Guardianship Orders, and six placed with kin who had been approved as long-term foster carers. One of the Special Guardianship Orders had been imposed by the court against the wishes of the local authority, which had recommended a stranger adoption because the kin were unable to protect the child from the birth parent. The social workers commented:

Cases are so complicated now. Our recommendations are not always agreed with, and this complicates the whole process.

Most (9) of these placements were thought by the responsible social worker to be the best placement for the child.

Long-term foster care (n = 3)

Three older children were in long-term foster care placements, and despite adoption recommendations, little had been done to find suitable adopters for two of them. One child, for example, had no active family finding for nine months, because her mother had not signed consent papers and there was no Care Order in place. During this time, she had had five foster care breakdowns, and it was decided that stability was now more important than ethnic matching. She was placed with white long-term foster carers, where she seemed to be doing well.

Summary

- Fifty children had a booking made for an adoption panel to consider whether an adoption recommendation should be made. The panel never saw 11 children's papers because plans had changed and decisions about three children were deferred because information was missing.
- Most of the social workers had found panel members supportive and had been pleased with the content of the meeting.
- Delays in family finding were because of a lack of court orders, incomplete or new kin assessments, and/or no family-finding workers having been allocated.
- Forty-two per cent of children had had a change of social worker since the panel made an adoption recommendation.
- At the final follow-up, 13 children had been placed for adoption, 19 were still waiting for a permanent placement, 11 were living with kin, four had been reunified, and three were in long-term foster care.
- Most of the adopted children had been placed in a two-parent heterosexual family, where there were other children.
- Social workers stated that some support was in place for 73 per cent of all adoptive parents but that most birth parents had declined support services.
- There had been very little promotion of the children still waiting for a permanent placement. Promotions, where they did occur, had happened sequentially.
- Some social workers were very pessimistic about children's chances of

being adopted, particularly those with a disability and older children.
- Mixed ethnicity children waiting for adoption were viewed as Black and their ethnicity was seen as a deterrent to potential adopters.

13 Summary and policy and practice pointers

In this final chapter, we summarise some of the main findings from the study and give some policy and practice suggestions for the future. Our aim is not to provide an exhaustive review of the data and the conclusions that may be drawn from them. Rather, we try to use the data to illuminate some of the big questions that arise in the complex matter of the placement of minority ethnic children with a view to permanence, and how the answers to these questions may help in the development of practice and policy. But first, a very brief review of the study and its design.

The study

The purpose of the study was to try to understand more about minority ethnic children's care pathways and to examine whether their placement outcomes were different from those of white children, especially in relation to permanence. We were interested in seeing whether differences and delays identified in previous research would be replicated with a larger sample of minority ethnic children and whether we could identify the processes and pathways that had contributed. For example, research using national data had found that minority ethnic children were less likely to be placed for adoption and waited longer at every stage of the process than white children (Ivaldi, 2000) but the reasons for the differences were unclear.

We designed the study in the context of many strongly-held beliefs and opinions about the placement of minority ethnic children but in the absence of little reliable evidence and data. Given this, it seemed advisable to collect data in a way that would make it possible to test some assumptions, but also to look for differences in the characteristics of children *within* the minority ethnic groups, as well as examining any differences in social work practice *between* groups. In order to have sufficient minority ethnic children for the "within group" analyses, we necessarily had to compromise on the size of the group of white children. The study should be seen as the *beginning* of research on issues of permanence for minority ethnic children, not an answer to all we might want to know.

Briefly, we selected three local authorities with high minority ethnic populations of different ethnicities. In each of these authorities, three samples were drawn in order to answer different questions.

The comparison sample of looked after white and minority ethnic children

This was a random sample of children under the age of 10 who had started to be looked after between 1 April 2002 and 31 March 2003, stratified on ethnicity (48 white and 54 of minority ethnicity). This sample was intended to answer questions about differences between white and minority ethnic children in their characteristics, entry to care, service use, decision-making, and placement outcomes. For example, some of our research questions were: in comparison with white children did minority ethnic children move towards permanence less frequently, more slowly or with poorer evaluation and assessment of needs?

Minority ethnic children with an adoption recommendation

We also wanted to see what differences there might be *between* different minority ethnic groups in their characteristics and what action followed an adoption recommendation. The comparison study did not provide sufficient numbers for this, so we drew a second sample of *all* the 120 minority ethnic children across our three authorities who had an adoption recommendation made between 1 April 2005 and 31 March 2006. Data were collected from children's files in exactly the same way as in the comparison study.

The interview sample

Finally, we wanted to understand more about the ways in which social workers took ethnicity into account when making difficult placement and matching decisions. To do this, a prospective real-time sample of 50 minority ethnic children, who were about to go to panel for an adoption recommendation between November 2005 and December 2006, was collected. Their social workers were interviewed before they presented their information to the panel and at subsequent monthly intervals to track the child's progress towards an adoptive placement. We were particularly interested in the way social workers thought about matching and the dilemmas they faced.

We can now consider what light the data from these three samples throw on some key questions about the way minority ethnic children become looked after and the decisions made about their futures. But first, it is necessary to consider who the minority ethnic children in these studies were.

Who were the minority ethnic children in these studies?

The most striking feature was the preponderance of children of mixed ethnicity in all the samples. In the comparison sample, 57 per cent of the minority ethnic children were of minority ethnicity; in the adoption recommended sample 69 per cent; and in the interview sample 74 per cent. The great majority of mixed ethnicity children had white mothers and were thus the outcome of relationships between white women and men from different ethnic backgrounds. Even mothers in the minority ethnic group, taken as a whole, sometimes came from mixed backgrounds (13% in the comparison sample and 20% in the adoption recommended sample).

It follows, from these data, that the groups of children who had two parents of African or of Asian origin in the comparison sample were small (13% and 30%). The smallest ethnic group in the adoption recommended sample was the black children (10%) and the proportion of children with both parents of Asian origin was also small (21%).

The issue of over- and under-representation of minority ethnic children who are looked after

There has been concern for some time about the over-representation of minority ethnic children amongst those who are looked after, that is, they make up a higher proportion of the looked after population than the base-rate for minority ethnic children in the population as a whole. Local demographics and majority and minority status influence whether children are under- or over-represented. For example, in our London borough, white children were over-represented in the looked after population (44% of the looked after population were white compared with 26% in the general population of that borough), because the large Bangladeshi group was so under-represented.

It has long been known that Asian children (Thoburn *et al*, 2000; Bebbington and Beecham, 2003) have been under-represented in those receiving family support, those on child protection registers, and those looked after, but the reasons for this are not well understood (Owen and Statham, 2009). For example, in our Northern authority, 23 per cent of children in the general population were of Pakistani heritage, but the proportion of the looked after population was only six per cent. Similarly, in the London borough, Bangladeshi children comprised 58 per cent of the total child population but only 17 per cent of the looked after population. With regard to African-Caribbean children, the picture was more complicated. In the Midland authority, which had the largest African-Caribbean child population, this group of children was also under-represented in the looked after population – two per cent looked after compared to four per cent in the population as a whole. This is different from the overall position in England where African-Caribbean children are somewhat over-represented (3% of looked after children compared to 1% of the child population).

Nationally, the percentage of mixed ethnicity looked after children has remained stable throughout 2002–2006 at eight per cent (DCSF, 2007) compared with a base-rate of three per cent in the general population, and they are thus over-represented in the looked after population. However, there are large regional differences in the proportions of mixed ethnicity children in the general population with, for example, mixed ethnicity children making up much larger proportions in inner London and Nottingham (Tikly *et al*, 2004).

Data from our authorities showed that mixed ethnicity children were especially over-represented in their looked after populations and were therefore over-represented in all our samples as well (Table 13.1).

Table 13.1
Over-representation of mixed ethnicity children in the looked after population in the three study authorities

Mixed ethnicity children	North	Midlands	London borough
Percentage in the child population[46]	3	8	5
As a % of all children looked after at year ending 31/3/02[47]	15	21	21

In practice, a mixed ethnicity group will contain children with a wide variety of ethnic heritages. For this reason, the characteristics of this group will depend on where the samples are drawn from. Because of this variation, it is unhelpful to refer to mixed ethnicity children as if they comprise a meaningful group or community.

This is well illustrated in the mixed ethnicity group in our largest sample of minority ethnic children with adoption recommendations. In the North, most (59%) of the mixed ethnicity children were of white/Asian parentage, whereas the majority were of white/Caribbean parentage in the Midlands (64%) and London (50%). This last figure might seem surprising for a London authority that has a large Asian population. However, the population in the borough is predominantly Bangladeshi but most of the mixed ethnicity children had Pakistani fathers. Moreover, about a quarter were children whose parents were from South-east Asia, Eastern Europe and China, and were categorised as "mixed other".

Because in our study the pathways of minority ethnic children for whom permanent alternative families are sought is predominantly a story of children with white mothers and minority ethnic fathers, it is necessary to see this within the context of mixed ethnicity in Britain more generally.

---

[46] Census 2001
[47] Data from the local authorities

Mixed ethnicity children

Mixed ethnicity children in the UK

The population of the UK is becoming increasingly diverse, with the fastest growing group being those who describe themselves on official forms as "mixed". However, mixed ethnicity children have remained invisible in social work policy and practice, partly because research has focused on looking at broad differences based on simple Black and White distinctions. A new wave of research (Parker and Song, 2001; Olumide, 2002; Ifekwunigwe, 2004; Tikly *et al*, 2004) has challenged the traditional view of the marginal or pathological nature of mixed ethnicity identities associated with the psychoanalytic tradition, and instead has emphasised the influence of social factors on identity development. This literature has also pointed out the dangers of treating the experiences of different categories of mixed ethnicity children as if they were the same. As a whole, the mixed ethnicity children's population has been found to be achieving well educationally (Bradford, 2006) but Tikly and colleagues' (2004) study of educational achievement in Birmingham found that white/African-Caribbean pupils as a group were doing less well than white pupils, while white/Asian pupils were outperforming all other groups at A levels. Interestingly, while this study found that children of white/African-Caribbean ethnicity came from more adverse backgrounds than other mixed groups, their poor performance was also influenced by teachers' stereotypical views about confused identities.

Research has not confirmed the stereotypes of social and identity problems. Caballero and colleagues (2009) found that many mixed ethnicity children were living in middle-class families and they were not facing daily battles around culture or ethnicity. Analysis of the Census 2001 found that mixed couples tended to be owner-occupiers, a high proportion had a degree or professional qualifications and over 50 per cent of mixed ethnicity children were living with both parents. However, Caballero and her colleagues did find that the experiences of families differed *within* as well as *between* mixed ethnicity groups and these experiences were strongly influenced by social class. For example, a middle-class white/Jamaican family did not necessarily have the same approach and experiences as those of a white/Jamaican working-class family and had sometimes more in common with a middle-class white/Asian family. Caballero's study has some important messages for social work practice. The authors comment on how thinking in the UK on issues of ethnicity has been influenced by ideas from the USA, which have stressed the "right" way to bring up Black children. In the study, parents used a range of approaches to parenting their mixed ethnicity children, with parenting strategies chosen to suit family circumstances. Some parents wanted their children to see their identity as open, some focused on a single aspect of their ethnicity, and others stressed the mix. There was no evidence that one approach led to better outcomes than another. Similarly, Tikly and colleagues (2004) found that mixed ethnicity pupils had a strong and positive sense of their own identity. Their identity problem, as such, was because they needed to have their identities recognised and understood in the school context.

Mixed ethnicity children in our study

There are a number of ways in which the mixed ethnicity children in our study were very different from the studies of these children in the general population. The children came from a small and very disadvantaged sub-group of those of mixed ethnicity, as is apparent in comparison with the studies quoted above. It is most important that the problems of our samples are not seen in any way to reflect, let alone typify, the lives and families of mixed ethnicity children in general.

The lives and families of our mixed ethnicity children were quite unlike those in the families studied by Caballero and her colleagues. For example, their sample included only two-parent families, whereas our children were more likely to be living with their white single mother and to have a father who had never been part of their lives. Many children had siblings of a different ethnicity. Indeed, in the adoption recommended sample, 75 per cent of all the mixed ethnicity children had a sibling with a different father. Moreover, their mothers, who were usually white, had had more problematic childhoods and had more adverse current circumstances than all other groups, including white mothers of white children. They also had high levels of alcohol and drug addiction, little extended family support, and were sometimes faced with overt racism or rejection from *within* their families, which led to the relinquishment of a child.

Because of this profile, about 25 per cent of all the mixed ethnicity children were born showing symptoms of FASD or neonatal abstinence syndrome, with consequent additional risks to healthy development, beyond the consequences of adverse parenting experiences. The vast majority of mixed ethnicity children were referred as infants, became looked after and had a "should be placed for adoption" recommendation made quickly. These children were more likely to be placed for adoption than black or Asian children and their chances of being adopted at older ages were higher than those of other minority ethnic children. In these respects, their pathways through the care system were similar to those of white children.

How did social workers think about mixed ethnicity children?

Social workers are required to give priority in placements to matching on or reflecting a child's ethnic heritage wherever possible. The interviews with them showed that they were especially struggling with how to consider matching mixed ethnicity children. The common approach taken (and often reported to be agency policy) was to view the children as "Black" and prioritise the ethnicity of the birth father. Social workers were confused about whether they should be placing a child to preserve his or her present identity or to enable the development of other minority ethnic identities to which the child had some genetic connection.

Because of this categorisation, long-term placements with white English foster carers and with white English adopters were seen as transracial and thought to be detrimental to a child's future development, especially in the construction of a healthy identity, problems which could lead to mental health difficulties later in life. However, interview and data from children's files suggested that skin colour did play a part in deciding the ethnicity of the child (when the father was unknown) and in determining the ethnicity of the family to be sought.

Mixed ethnicity children were also described by social workers as "hard to place", although the focus on ethnicity as a problem was not associated with the children having known or potential developmental problems. Thinking of the child as "hard to place" was surprising in some ways, as the children were usually very young and therefore ought to have been amongst the easiest for whom to find families. Thinking of these children as difficult seemed mostly associated with problems in matching. It is, therefore, useful at this point to give an account of how social workers thought about culture and ethnicity.

How did social workers think about culture and ethnicity more generally?

There has been very little previous research (Williams and Soyden, 2005) about how social workers in England think about culture and ethnicity. The social workers we interviewed used the term ethnicity interchangeably with culture. When talking about culture, they were often referring only to ethnic categorisations, even though crude ethnic labels did not necessarily help in understanding a child's culture. There was also a tendency to see the categories of Black and White as fixed, whereas we know culture is constantly changing and dynamic.

Of course, a social worker might have a keen appreciation of culture and cultural needs, even if she or he was not adept at abstract discussion of ethnicity and culture, so we searched the children's files for recording of culture, language, religion and identity. We looked particularly for the elements identified in the Integrated Children's System, such as whether a child was given the opportunity to learn their own cultural traditions and language or eat familiar food, but there was so little recorded that analysis was impossible. The part of the Assessment Framework that should have provided information about the child's home, community and cultural background was often blank or had a few formulaic sentences. It was not possible to know, for example, whether the birth mothers of mixed ethnicity children had chosen to live in an ethnically diverse area or whether they were living in a predominantly white working-class area. There was virtually no information on the files about the children's earlier cultural experiences, for example, the food they were used to, festivals celebrated, or religious observances. This supports similar findings from an earlier study of the Assessment Framework (Cleaver and Walker, 2004).

Is it helpful to think of all minority ethnic children as Black?

It was common amongst the social workers we interviewed to think of all minority ethnic children as Black, a view common in the social work field more generally. The most powerful justification for this is that society itself uses this broad classification, which has a profound influence on the way that all those with darker skins are treated. Focusing on Black issues has been successful in raising political and professional awareness of the needs of minority ethnic children arising from oppression resulting from racism and racist discrimination, and consequently drawing attention to some of the problems transracially adopted children have faced. Black as an identifier has forged a broad consensus around the need for greater equality and forced recognition of discrimination, racism and prejudice. However, increasingly writers have challenged this position because it reduces culture to a single entity (Gilroy, 1990; Macey, 1995) and there is a perception that some Black cultures are more valued than others. For example, Modood and colleagues (1997) remarked, 'When Asians are encouraged to think of themselves as Black . . . they have to redefine themselves in a framework that is historically and internationally developed by people in search of African roots'. For some minority ethnic groups, understanding the impact of colonialism is of more relevance than understanding the legacy of slavery.

Recent research in many fields has identified that within minority ethnic groups there are different barriers to educational achievement or to good health and therefore different strategies are needed to overcome these. For example, in education, providing mentors and supplementary educational opportunities are often effective at raising the achievement of African-Caribbean pupils, while providing targeted language support is important for raising the achievement of many pupils of South Asian origin (Tikly et al, 2004). Similarly, in health, the NHS has begun to develop specialisms in ethnic health. Their on-line library (www.library. nhs.uk/ethnicity) provides available evidence on the specific health needs of different minority groups and best methods of service delivery. Disadvantage and discrimination also need to be understood through the wider lens of gender, social class and faith. In education, research has examined how African-Caribbean boys develop 'undesirable learner identities' (Sewell *et al*, 1998; Youdell, 2003) and the important role of faith in shaping the experiences and identities of male Muslim pupils (Archer, 2003). Racism, because it is socially constructed, is fluid, and increasingly in Britain, religion is seen as an important marker of difference. Therefore, it is important to recognise that some children may be more at risk than others. In a small study (Woods, 2008), Somali black Muslim boys were the victims of the most racist incidents in a London primary school.

One consequence of the view that all minority ethnic children are Black has been an emphasis on placing minority ethnic children with Black adopters, because it is thought that they, irrespective of their cultural or ethnic backgrounds, will be better able to help the children deal with racism. We know very little about how parents prepare and support their children in a racist society and there is little strong research evidence to back this assumption (Quinton, 2010). Indeed, children of mixed ethnicity can face hostility from Black and White children and adults, being seen as different, rather than as sharing the same cultures (Alibhai-Brown and Montague, 1992; Twine, 1999; Tikly *et al*, 2004). So, while it is important to recognise the difficulties all Black children face, particularly the common experience of racism, it is important to look at children's individual histories and needs and develop individualised care planning.

Recent studies have shown that minority ethnic parents do not always know how to support their children and challenge racism (Scourfield *et al*, 2002; Twine, 2004). In the few studies available, first generation immigrants were reported as having more difficulties, as they were unprepared for the variety of forms racism takes, lacked a vocabulary for discussing racism, and often had the desire to fit in and not complain. In our study, some minority ethnic adopters stated that their preferred method of dealing with racism was to ignore it, but we know from children's accounts (Connolly, 1998) and research (Barter, 1999) that this is not usually a successful strategy. Moreover, white English adopters were not expected to adopt minority ethnic children but some did so knowingly, and others may have done so when the ethnicity of a child was unknown. Yet, few placements had planned support and advice on racism.

The pathways to permanence for minority ethnic and white children

The discussion so far has highlighted the complexities in drawing conclusions about differences between the care pathways of children based on simple ethnic categories. It is, therefore, with some trepidation that we now attempt to draw some conclusions on some important issues concerning the care pathways of minority ethnic and white children, using the simple divisions of ethnicity against which we have cautioned.

Earlier research (Barn, 1993; Barn and Sinclair, 2001) suggested that minority ethnic children enter care more rapidly and have different patterns of agency referral than white children. This is important, so we begin with this issue, using the data from all the samples. We look first at the initial referral stage, then at the children and families once the children became looked after, and finally as they progressed towards permanence.

Referral to children's services

Who referred them?

If there was systematic differential activity in interventions with minority ethnic children and their families, then we might expect them to come to the notice of Children's Services at a younger age and, indeed, be more likely to be referred by Children's Services themselves than by other agencies.

There were no simple differences of this sort. White *and* mixed ethnicity children were *more* likely to have been referred by Children's Services than black and Asian children, usually because the mothers of these white or mixed ethnicity children were already on the caseloads of social workers who were involved because of other children in the family. In contrast, black and Asian families were more likely to refer themselves or to be referred by education services or by their own families.

At referral, black children were on average much older than white, mixed ethnicity or Asian children. However, the sample of black children was very small. The census categorisation puts together those of recent African origin and those from the Caribbean. In this study's small black samples, African-Caribbean children were UK born second or third generation, whereas the African children were often older and first generation, were moving between countries (which delayed interventions) and were sometimes in private fostering arrangements. These factors led to later referral.

Why were they referred?

Differences in the reasons for referral are another possible indicator that Children's Services are taking more precipitate action in the case of one ethnic group than another. There were high levels of abuse and neglect in all the samples but children with white or mixed ethnicity mothers were more likely to be referred for neglect, while black children were often referred for physical abuse, and Asian children because their family was experiencing acute stress and there was the potential for abuse or neglect. Again, this might be a consequence of black children being older when they were first referred, with neglect being seen as of greater concern for infants. Mental health problems and domestic violence were equally prevalent in minority ethnic and white families.

Was the initial service response different?

Domestic violence was prevalent in all the families but there seemed to be few services available to deal with this. Rather, social work interventions focused on maternal neglect, without the back-up of adult services to tackle the related problem of domestic violence. There were no differences in the number or type of agencies involved with white or minority ethnic families. However, the lack of services more generally was not just a problem of availability. Forty-two per cent of the birth parents of minority ethnic children refused services or failed to turn up for appointments. It was not possible from children's file data to know whether this was because of culturally inappropriate services being offered, language barriers, or the lifestyle and choices that parents had made.

Were there family differences between the white and minority ethnic groups at referral?

Another possible indicator of the differential treatment of white and minority ethnic families is differences in the characteristics of the parents of white and minority ethnic children. If the latter were more precipitately referred and/or taken into the care system more easily, then we might expect their family profiles to be less problematic than those of white families or for action to be taken more quickly for white and minority ethnic families with similar profiles. Since the parenting circumstances and capacities of mothers are a key element in this, we briefly review the differences between them.

White and mixed ethnicity mothers

White mothers and mothers who were themselves of mixed ethnicity had profiles of similar disadvantages, although the mothers of mixed ethnicity had experienced the most adversity. They were more likely to have been in care themselves, to have been abused and neglected, and to be alcohol or drug dependent. The childhood experiences and adult difficulties for the white and mixed ethnicity mothers are very striking. They show up the failures of social provision and support when the mothers in this group were themselves children. As a consequence of their problems with substance misuse, their newborn babies were the most likely to have FASD or neonatal abstinence syndrome. There were also examples of white mothers who relinquished their mixed ethnicity infants because of overt racism within their own families.

The mothers (usually white) who had mixed ethnicity children had the lowest levels of extended family support and were more likely to be single parents than the mothers of white, Asian or black children. Unlike the earlier research by Barn and colleagues (1997), the fathers of mixed ethnicity children in our samples were not predominantly African-Caribbean men, but were also of Asian, especially Pakistani, ethnicity. Of course, this was related to our choice of local authority areas and illustrates how regional differences can affect a sample.

Asian and black mothers

Many of the Asian and black mothers were not born in the UK: 38 per cent in the comparison sample and 48 per cent in the adoption recommended sample. Many Asian babies were relinquished and the concept of honour (*izzat*) played a significant part in this decision. Some Asian mothers felt the shame brought on themselves and their family was so great that the child had to be relinquished. Neil (2000) first noted this pattern of relinquishment, and the role of *izzat* has also been identified in relation to the reluctance to report child abuse (NSPCC, 2007). A few mothers were subject to domestic violence by extended family members during their pregnancy and feared for their lives if they did not relinquish the child. Social workers in these cases were in a difficult position. If they revealed any of the details of the mother and her child, then the mother's life might be in danger, but if they accepted the position at face value, there was no opportunity to test out the extended family's wishes. This dilemma was illustrated in one case in the interview sample, where the child was reunified with her mother after the family found out about the birth and did not react as the mother had expected.

Comments on the initial referral of children and families

The summary given above does not lead to the conclusion of a systematic differential identification and service response to children and families of different ethnicities. Rather, there was a complex set of reasons for those differences that did exist, none of which characterised white and minority ethnic differences as a whole, but rather pointed to a variety of specific issues for each group.

It should be remembered that our sampling strategy only included children who became looked after. It therefore follows that the same conclusions cannot be drawn for minority ethnic children who are "in need" but who do not go on to be looked after.

Being looked after

Ethnic differences between white and minority ethnic children and within the minority ethnic group might become more apparent once children become looked after. Reception into care might happen more speedily for minority ethnic children, or the action might be taken with less evidence, or taken with families with less problematic profiles. However, lack of difference continued when we looked at the timing of receptions into care. There were no differences between the ethnic groups in the length of time from first referral to first becoming looked after. Neither was there any evidence of either greater delay or speed in taking minority ethnic children into care.

Foster placement history

The samples were primarily of very young children. We did not expect to find a great deal of movement in foster placements, since placement disruption is usually related to challenging behaviour at later ages, although Ward *et al* (2003) found frequent movement to be quite common for looked after babies as well. Placement stability in our comparison sample was quite good (7% of minority ethnic children and 15% of white children experiencing a foster care disruption) but a quarter of children in the adoption recommended sample experienced a disruption. These mostly occurred because of the retirement of the foster carer, a euphemism for the ending of the working relationship between the foster carer and the local authority.

Most Asian children were in foster placements that matched their ethnicity. However, there was a tendency to match against the broad category of Asian rather than considering the distinct needs of Indian, Pakistani and Bangladeshi children. Mixed ethnicity children were usually placed with white English foster carers, but black children were unlikely to be in a matched foster placement. Social workers made great efforts to keep siblings together. In the adoption recommended sample, 88 per cent of children with siblings were placed with brothers and/or sisters in foster care.

Adoption recommendations and the adoption process

Overall, there were no statistical differences by the child's ethnicity in plans for placement. Somewhat more white than minority ethnic children were recommended for adoption, although this difference was not statistically significant. This is in line with Sinclair *et al*'s (2007) finding that the majority of young entrants to the care system are considered for adoption.

The white and mixed ethnicity children went to panel at the same age on average, the Asian children somewhat later, and the black children were the oldest at panel, again reflecting the fact that they were older when they first came to the attention of Children's Services. However, the Asian and black children did spend statistically longer being looked after before the recommendation for adoption was made. Delayed decision-making was more likely when the family was not previously known to Children's Services.

How well were the children's needs and circumstances assessed?

A number of key assessment documents ought to be available when the case is referred to the adoption panel. These include the core assessment, the Adoption Medical and the Form E (Child Permanence Report). Adequate decision making for children of all ethnicities depends on the quality of the assessments made of their physical, psychosocial and cultural needs. One of the major findings from this study is the worryingly poor quality of – or lack of – documented assessments. This finding supports the conclusions of the Conceptual and Research review of Matching (Quinton, forthcoming), where the assessment of children's needs seems to have received very little attention, in comparison with the assessment of potential adopters.

Core assessment: Many children had important documents missing from their files. Completed core assessments were absent for about half the white and mixed ethnicity children and were even less common for the black and Asian ones. There was even less assessment activity for children who were later reunified and for those who had their plans changed away from adoption. This might be a consequence of the lack of independent scrutiny of permanence plans that do not reach an adoption or permanence panel. There was no indication on files that the Independent Reviewing Officer was questioning inadequate assessments.

Adoption assessments: Even when a decision had been made that a child should be considered for adoption, adoption medicals were missing significantly more often from the files of black and Asian children. Assessments of children's health and emotional and behavioural needs were also poorly articulated in the Form E or Child's Permanence Report (CPR), particularly for minority ethnic children. There was little analysis of the early adverse environments the children had experienced and the likely impact of these on the child, his or her emotional or behavioural development, or on the supports needed to help adopters.

A number of factors contributed to poor assessment: the wish for a "same-race" placement dominated Form E/CPR descriptions over and above other needs; frequent changes of social worker led to a lack of knowledge about the child and often to the case being taken over by inexperienced workers; and there was an underlying view that infants did not have needs other than basic physical ones, and a wish not to "label" the child and make them "hard to place" by being specific about potential problems.

Kin assessment: There was, however, a great deal of assessment activity while children were looked after and during family finding concerned with trying to find kin placements – another requirement of recent legislation. About three-quarters of all the children had at least one extended family member assessed for their suitability to care. Many kin assessments took place sequentially, sometimes because family members came forward one after the other, and sometimes because social workers wanted to check each relative's suitability before moving on to the next assessment. Delays inevitably followed, especially when assessments were undertaken outside the UK. In other cases, new members of the extended family continued to come forward asking to care for the child right up to the making of the Adoption Order. This was sometimes viewed as a delaying tactic. Social workers were often instructed by the courts to undertake more kin assessments, even though they "took the view" that these were unlikely to be successful.

While assessments were ongoing, family-finding activity stopped. Most assessments found that extended family members were not able to care for the child. In the comparison sample, only 15 per cent were placed with kin (just two of these children were placed with kin for adoption), and in the adoption recommended sample, four per cent were adopted by kin and three per cent placed with kin as long-term foster carers.

Effect of social work changes on assessment and family finding: The assessment process was also affected by the fact that social workers frequently changed. In the interview sample, the average length of time the social worker had known the child was eight months, with more than a third having met the child fewer than four weeks before the research interview.

Many children's social workers knew very little about the adoption process. Sometimes this was because they were a new member of staff and sometimes because another team took over family finding once the adoption decision had been made. Even so, children's social workers continued to carry case responsibility, including writing the child's profile, meeting with the prospective adopters, and ensuring that the necessary paperwork had been completed.

Three-quarters of these workers expected to continue working with the child and to see them into their adoptive placement. However, at follow-up, only 29 (59%) of the original 49 social workers were still working with the child and some children had had two or more social workers since the panel had made its recommendation. It was also not obvious from children's files if anyone was actively family finding when social workers were off sick for long periods or where there were gaps before a new social worker was appointed. There has rightly been a great deal of emphasis on improving the stability of placements for children, but it is important to recognise that to achieve this, the workforce too needs to be stable.

Which children with adoption recommendations found adoptive placements?

By the end of our data collection, 83 per cent of the white children were in adoptive placements, 69 per cent of those of mixed ethnicity, 42 per cent of the black children and 36 per cent of the Asian children. The black and Asian children who were adopted were younger at referral, when they became looked after and at the time of the panel recommendation, when compared with the mixed ethnicity children. Only black and Asian children under three years old had been found adoptive families and the majority (60%) of Asian children and 42 per cent of the black children had had their adoption plan rescinded. White and mixed ethnicity children were more likely to be adopted and to be adopted at older ages – up to the age limit in our sample of 10 years old.

Most children were placed in-house. There was a drop in the number of children placed with Voluntary Adoption Agencies (VAAs) from 19 per cent in the comparison sample to six per cent in the adoption recommended sample. It is surprising that VAAs were not used more, as some specialise in finding placements for minority ethnic children.

Multivariate analyses showed that age and ethnicity were the big determinants of adoptive placements. Infants were ten times more likely to be adopted than a child older than three years at the time of the panel recommendation, and mixed ethnicity children were four times more likely to be adopted than Asian children. The average time from the recommendation for adoption to placement with an adoptive family for all minority ethnic children was 12 months. However, many minority ethnic children had their plan changed away from adoption if no adopters had been found within six months. Efforts to place white children continued for longer.

Most of the minority ethnic children in adoptive placements were exactly or partially matched by ethnicity (80% black, 78% Asian, and 85% mixed ethnicity). Black children were more likely to be in an ethnically matched adoptive placement than a foster care placement. Eighty-one per cent of the Muslim and 57 per cent of the Christian children were in placements exactly matched by faith, and all were matched by language.

Placement outcomes in the interview sample

The prospective interview study was designed to follow through what happened to minority ethnic children as they went to panel and subsequently. In practice, 22 per cent of the children in the interview sample had their plan changed away from adoption in the few weeks *leading up to* the panel booking. Panel time is precious, so it is concerning that so much booked time was wasted. In this sample, some children had triple-track plans with adoption being just one of several options. Some delays in taking cases to panel were driven by court decisions that there should be more kin assessments. Some social workers felt that courts were increasingly willing to challenge the adoption panel's recommendation and the social work plan. The influence of the courts on decision-making was far more evident when talking to social workers than when reading their reports on children's files.

The placement outcomes for the 50 children in the interview sample, at the end of data collection, were disheartening. Only 13 had been placed for adoption, 19 were still waiting, 11 had been placed with kin, three were in long-term foster care and three had gone back home. There seemed little prospect of adoption for most of the waiting children, since they were not being promoted and their social workers were pessimistic about the likelihood of adoption.

Finding adopters for minority ethnic children

Minority ethnic children had fewer prospective adopters showing interest in them in comparison with white children. Even very young minority ethnic infants often had just one or two possible new families. This limited pool of potential adopters for minority ethnic children arose for a number of reasons: first, community demographics simply meant that there were fewer minority ethnic adults than white adults in the community, even when minority ethnic children made up a substantial part of the child population; secondly, limited or no promotion of the child; thirdly, because of social workers' negativity/pessimism about adoption; and finally, due to a concentration on "same-race" placements.

Asian and black prospective adopters were in short supply, and therefore were able to turn down children who did not meet their prefer-ences. With more minority ethnic children needing placement and few adopters, potential minority ethnic adopters were able to select the young-est children with little or no apparent difficulties. Many Asian adopters did not want to adopt mixed ethnicity children. There was also some evidence from the qualitative analysis of Children's Services' records of a reluctance to use potential adopters who were in an ethnically mixed relationship. It was also surprising that, for many children's social workers, their "ideal" adoptive family was an ethnically matched two-parent family with children, and who were financially secure. Qualities of warmth, commitment, and ability to manage the child's needs were a lower priority.

Promotion and profiles

Family-finding activity was generally sequential. Workers first looked in-house, then through the consortium, then to other local authorities, after which VAAs were approached for some children. Not all children were promoted beyond the consortium. Where children were promoted, more potential adopters were identified and there was greater choice. However, the likelihood of promotion was related to agency practice not the child's age or special needs. Writing profiles is an art and sometimes these were poorly written and often stressed the complexity of a child's ethnicity and asked for an adoptive family that could meet all the child's cultural and developmental needs. Meeting these needs in other ways did not seem to be considered, such as linking the adoptive family into specific communities or providing a mentor. In the general population, families look to aunts, uncles, grandparents, or family friends to provide experiences that they cannot, but in adoption practice, prospective adopters often seem to be expected to provide everything. Consequently, some children were never placed.

Adoption support

Support was not planned for most placements until the identity of the adopters was known, and so we have few data on the kind and quality of adoption support that was put in place. However, the lack of good assessments of the children makes it likely that support for children's problems will be reactive rather than proactive. Children's social workers were hopeful that support would be provided but not all adopters and children were thought to need it.

Not surprisingly, very few birth parents received any support, given how few had engaged with services over years of involvement with the authority. It is unlikely that birth parents will accept local authority services at the time of an adoption, if they have never done so in the past. However, the provision of an independent worker for the birth parent seemed to come quite late in the process: after the adoption recommendation had been made. Perhaps, if appointed earlier, there might be a greater likelihood of engaging parents with the adoption process.

Professional disagreements

"Transracial" placements: A major source of professional disputes was the requests by foster carers to adopt minority ethnic children in their care. In most instances, this involved white English foster carers who had been caring for a mixed ethnicity child since or shortly after birth. Social workers tried to decide between the benefits of the child's attachment on the one hand and the presumed damage to identity and self-esteem on the other. Since mixed ethnicity children were viewed as Black, it was argued that they should be moved to a matched placement for the sake of their mental health. This conflict was regularly heard during lengthy proceedings in the courts, during which numerous expert witnesses were called. In all the cases where this occurred in this sample, judgement went in favour of the foster carer. Unfortunately, the battle left the relationships between the carer and the authority in disarray. In this climate, children who might well benefit from specific support around ethnicity, culture and identity might be lucky to have this put in place.

There is research evidence (Rutter, 1989; Black, 2000) that shows that young children do badly when attachment bonds are disrupted. Children can be moved when it is inevitable, such as when a parent dies or away from an abusive environment, but it is difficult to justify moving a child from a secure good foster home (where the carer is asking to adopt or offering a permanent home) on the grounds of future possible benefit. Rutter (1989), stressing a developmental perspective on separation, wrote:

> *Thus very young children are protected from separation experiences*
> *because they have yet to develop strong attachments; older children*
> *are protected because they have learned to maintain relationships*

over time and space, but toddlers are most at risk because attachments first become established at that age and because they lack the cognitive skills required to maintain relationships during absence. (p 273)

However, some workers took the view that, if children had already been able to form a secure attachment, they would quickly be able to form another. The child's subsequent stress and confusion were underestimated, particularly for children who had known no other mother, and lacked the vocabulary to understand and express feelings, and where familiar carers were unavailable to provide comfort. Studies have found that the risk of developing a depressive illness in adolescence or adult life is doubled if one loses a parent figure before the age of ten years and the risk for children under four years of age is four to five times higher (Black, 2000).

Sibling placements: Professional disagreements also arose over sibling adoptive placements, especially when different social workers held case responsibility for the children. Sometimes children's social workers wanted to give the youngest child the chance of adoption by splitting the sibling group or a worker wanted to split a sibling group because the children had fathers of different ethnicity. This sometimes led to professional disagreement between the children's social workers and the family placement teams. This was surprising as it was clear from file recording that extensive efforts had gone into keeping siblings together in foster care.

Unusual parental beliefs: Social workers also experienced conflicts and confusion in cases where birth parents had superstitious beliefs that had led to the child suffering serious physical abuse and torture. In a few Asian and African families (5), the parents believed that the child was a witch or a sorcerer, or harboured demons and needed to be punished, feared and be subject to exorcism. Notes on children's files showed that some local religious leaders supported these beliefs and had led ceremonies to rid children of their "evil". These cases shared some common features with that of Victoria Climbié. Social workers struggled to work with parents in these circumstances, as behaviours appeared bizarre and the abuse was outside the terms of reference or experience of most workers. It was only when cases went to court that experts in particular cultures were called, who could explain the parents' thinking, and this helped the social worker develop a plan of intervention. Social workers cannot be expected to know all there is to know about every culture and religion in the world and therefore it is important that they should be able to access information and advice when needed. This may not come from sources social workers have traditionally drawn upon and instead might include anthropologists or those studying religion.

Comment on ethnic similarities and differences

This final chapter has concentrated on setting out the most important differences and similarities between ethnic groups in becoming looked after and in the children's pathways to permanence via adoption. We commented first on the crudity of ethnic classifications, including those used in the Census and other official data-gathering exercises, let alone on the crudity of a binary division between Black and White. We were, nevertheless, constrained to use a broad white, black, Asian and mixed categorisation in our analyses and further work needs to be undertaken to look at children's different experiences within these broad categories.

The first thing we would want to emphasis is the small size of black[48] and Asian populations amongst those looked after and their under-representation in our study, compared with children of mixed ethnicity. Children of mixed ethnicity were by far the largest minority ethnic group and were over-represented in all three of our local authorities, in which white children were sometimes over-represented as well.

The conclusion here is that it makes no sense to talk about or to research minority ethnic children in the care system as if they were a homogeneous group. Indeed, it is unhelpful to talk about "Asian" or "black" children either, since the profiles and experiences of the former differ greatly depending on whether their origins lie in Bangladesh or Pakistan or India, and of the latter on whether they are of African-

---

[48] Black children are slightly over-represented in the looked after population nationally, but 69% are over 10 years of age and therefore are unlikely to have an adoption recommendation.

Caribbean origin or have recently arrived from one of the countries in Africa.

The characteristics of the children's families and their own childhood experiences showed more similarities than differences. In short, there was no "big" story about systematic bias against or mishandling of minority ethnic children compared with white children from the time they came to the attention of Children's Services, nor any story about a tendency to take minority ethnic children into care more precipitately. Nevertheless, there were a number of important differences that highlight social work hesitance or even confusion about how to address the interests of minority ethnic children, especially those of black or Asian heritage.

The black children came to the notice of Children's Services when they were older than the white, Asian or mixed ethnicity children and, therefore, they were older when they first became looked after. This age difference affected their subsequent care pathways, so that they were much less likely than the white or mixed ethnicity children to progress towards adoption. It must be emphasised again that this is a small group with particular histories and needs, especially in the case of the African children.

The Asian children showed few significant differences from the white and mixed ethnicity children in terms of the age at which they came to the notice of Children's Services. The most striking difference in their case was the role played by *izzat* (family honour) in the impetus to relinquish or abandon children, rather than the more familiar pattern of poor parenting experiences, parents' childhoods spent in care, family break-down and substance misuse. It should be emphasised that the high proportion for whom *izzat* was an issue in this study may well be sample specific. It should not be concluded that this is a problem that applies equally to Asian women in all local authority areas.

Our three local authorities had different minority ethnic populations and practice was noticeably different in the London borough. Children in the London borough had more reunification plans and had more kin assessments. Asian and black children were referred at older ages and waited longer for adoption recommendations than white or mixed ethnicity children in that borough and longer than black and Asian children in the other two authorities. The borough used more promotion than the other two authorities and found adopters mainly for the young mixed ethnicity children.

The likelihood of adoption for the black and Asian children was low in all three authorities, with plans changing away from adoption for the majority of the latter group. The ostensible reason was a failure to find suitable adopters – presumably a matching issue – or a decision that a current non-adoptive placement best served the child's needs. These problems in securing adoptive placements may have arisen predominantly because of an over-rigid application of matching rules, but other evidence points to a greater level of social workers' insecurity in decision-making for the black and Asian children, over and above matching problems.

First, there was evidence of more delay in permanency decisions for black and Asian children, when they were looked after. Secondly, the quality of information gathered on them – for example, core assessments and adoption medicals or health plans – was especially poor; indeed, it was not good for any ethnic group, including white children. Thirdly, the use of promotion in an attempt to find carers for these children was low and, finally, there was worrying evidence in the interview sample that social workers very quickly became pessimistic about the likelihood of finding adopters for many minority ethnic children with adoption recommendations.

Matching

There is a lack of good evidence (Quinton, forthcoming) on what constitutes a good match and whether this makes any difference to psychosocial outcomes, especially identity, in the long run. Studies in the USA have found that disruption rates for matched and non-matched children are much the same and that there are few differences on most psychosocial outcomes or self-esteem. A review by the Evan B. Donaldson Institute (2009) concluded that the available research evidence suggests that "transracial" adoption does not, in itself, produce psychological or behavioural problems in children but those who adopt "transracially" face a range of additional challenges. The way in which adoptive parents handle those challenges facilitates or hinders their child's psychosocial development. This finding supports UK and USA research (Evan B. Donaldson Institute, 2009; McRoy, 2009; Quinton, forthcoming) that has highlighted the importance of the commitment, flexibility, open communication, humour and willingness of adopters to work with the agencies, as the ingredients of a successful adoption.

This is not to suggest that the ethnicity and culture of children should be ignored. We have stressed a consistent research finding that virtually all minority ethnic children are subject to racism and for many children a placement matched on ethnicity will be in their best interests. It will be where children feel comfortable. Many adoption agencies, however, have difficulty in finding an "exact" ethnically matched placement for a child. The UK population is becoming increasingly diverse and the complexity of mixed ethnicity relationships makes it increasingly unlikely that "exact" matches will be able to be found. Even if matched by a broad ethnic category, families may differ culturally because of social class and neighbourhoods. While far more efforts need to be made to recruit as wide and diverse a pool of adopters as possible, there also needs to be greater realism about the likelihood of finding a "perfect ethnic match". Most of the children with adoption recommendations are of mixed ethnicity, with complex histories, carrying with them many risk factors for delayed development. Deciding what a "same-race" placement is for a mixed ethnicity child is fraught with difficulties. Therefore, we suggest that a more sensitive and sophisticated approach to assessment, matching and placement is required.

Adopters also need to be better prepared to challenge racism and to become more culturally competent. There are a number of training models offered in the US (Vonk, 2001) but we do not know if these are appropriate for the UK and this is an area that needs urgent attention. There is a need for much greater subtlety and differentiation in research and practice in our understanding of ethnicity and culture and how this relates to the past experiences, attachments and future development of minority ethnic children. This study, we hope, will be followed by many others that will examine in greater detail the differences within the minority ethnic group and the strategies that need to be put into place to help children in their placements.

References

Adoption Register for England and Wales (2006) *Annual Report*, London: Adoption Register

Ahmed B. (1990) *Black Perspectives in Social Work*, Birmingham: Venture Press

Alam M. Y. and Husband C. (2006) *British-Pakistani Men from Bradford: Linking narratives to policy*, York: Joseph Rowntree Foundation

Alibhai-Brown Y. and Monatague A. (1992) *The Colour of Love*, London: Virago

Archer L. (2003) *Race, Masculinity and Schooling: Muslim boys and education*, Berkshire: Open University Press

Avery R. (2000) 'Perceptions and practice: agency efforts for the hardest-to-place children', *Children and Youth Services Review*, 22:6, pp 399–420

BAAF (2003) *Response to Review of Research on Child Welfare Services for Children of Minority Ethnic Origin and their Families*, London: BAAF. Available at www.baaf.org.uk

BAAF (2007) *Chief Executive's Report* 17/05/07

Banks N. (1995) 'Children of black mixed parentage and their placement needs', *Adoption & Fostering*, 19:2, pp 9–24

Barn R. (1993) *Black Children in the Public Care System*, London: Batsford

Barn R., Ladino C. and Rogers B. (2006) *Parenting in Multiracial Britain*, York: Joseph Rowntree Foundation

Barn R. and Sinclair R. (2001) 'Black families and children: planning to meet their needs', *Research Policy and Planning*, 17:2, pp 5–11

Barn R., Sinclair R. and Ferdinand D. (1997) *Acting on Principle: An examination of race and ethnicity in social services provision for children and families*, London: BAAF

Barter C. (1999) *Protecting Children from Racism and Racial Abuse: A research review*, London: NSPCC

Bebbington A. and Beecham J. (2003) *Children in Need 2001: Ethnicity and service use*, Canterbury: PSSRU

Bebbington A. and Miles J. (1989) 'The background of children who enter local authority care', *British Journal of Social Work*, 19:5, pp 349–368

Becher H. and Husain F. (2003) *Supporting Minority Ethnic Families: South Asian Hindu and Muslims in Britain – developments in family support*, London: NFPI

Bernard C. and Gupta A. (2006) 'Black African children and the child protection system', *British Journal of Social Work*, 38:3, pp 476–492

Bhopal R. (2004) 'Glossary of terms relating to ethnicity and race: for reflection and debate', *Journal of Epidemiol Community Health*, 58:6, pp 441–445

Black D. (2000) 'The effects of bereavement in childhood', in Gelder M., Lopez-Ibor M. and Andreason N. (eds) *New Oxford Textbook of Psychiatry*, Oxford: Oxford University Press

Bradford B. (2006) *Who are the 'Mixed' Ethnic Group?*, London: ONS

Brandon M., Belderson P., Warren C., Howe D., Gardner R., Dodsworth J. and Black J. (2008) *Analysing Child Deaths and Serious Injury through Abuse and Neglect: What can we learn?*, Sheffield: DCSF, Research report DCSF-RR023

Brophy J., Jhutti-Johal J. and Owen C. (2003) 'Assessing and documenting child ill-treatment in ethnic minority households', *Family Law*, 33, pp 756–764

Caballero C., Edwards R. and Puthussery S. (2009) *Parenting 'Mixed' Children: Difference and belonging in mixed race and faith families*, York: Joseph Rowntree Foundation. Available at www.jrf.org.uk

Chahal K. and Julienne L. (1999) *'We Can't all be White! Racist victimisation in the UK*, York: Joseph Rowntree Foundation

Chand A. and Thoburn J. (2005) 'Research review: child and family support services with minority ethnic families: what can we learn from research?', *Child and Family Social Work*, 10:2, pp 169–178

Channer Y. and Parton N. (1990) 'Racism, cultural relativism and child protection', in The Violence against Study Group, *Taking Child Abuse Seriously*, London: Unwin Hyman

Cleaver H. and Walker S. (2004) *Assessing Children's Needs and Circumstances: The impact of the Assessment Framework*, London: Jessica Kingsley Publishers

Cohen J., Deblinger E., Mannarino A. and Arellano M. (2001) 'The importance of culture in treating abused and neglected children: an empirical review', *Child Maltreatment*, 6:2, pp 148–157

Collier F., Hutchinson B., and Pearman J. (2000) *Linking Children with Adoptive Parents: Messages from a review of BAAF's national family-finding services*, London: BAAF

Connolly P. (1998) *Racism, Gender Identities and Young Children Social Relations in a Multi-Ethnic, Inner City Primary School*, London: Routledge

Corby B. (1993) *Child Abuse*, Milton Keynes: Open University Press

Cornell S. (1996) 'The variable ties that bind: content and circumstances in ethnic processes', *Ethnic and Racial Studies*, 19:2, pp 265–89

Cousins J. (2003) 'Are we missing the match?', *Adoption & Fostering*, 27:4, pp 7–18

Creighton S. J. (1992) *Child Abuse Trends in England and Wales 1988–1990*, London: NSPCC

Crippen C. and Brew L. (2007) 'Inter-cultural parenting and the trans-cultural family: a literature review', *The Family Journal*, 15:2, pp 107–115

Department for Children, Schools and Families (2007) *Table 4D: Children and Young People on Child Protection Registers at 1st March 2006 by Ethnic Origin*, London: DCSF. Available at www.dfes.gov.uk

Department for Children, Schools and Families (2008) *Statistical First Release: Children looked after in England year ending 31st March 2008*, London: DCSF, SFR/2008

Department for Children, Schools and Families (2009) *Statistical First Release: Children Looked after in England year ending 31st March 2009*, SFR25/2009

Department for Communities and Local Government (2006) *Connecting British Hindus*, London: Runnymede Trust, commissioned by the Hindu Forum of Britain

Department of Health (1998) *Adoption: Achieving the right balance*, London: Department of Health, Circular LAC (98) 20

Department of Health (2002) *Adoption Statistics Bulletin 2002/22*, London: Department of Health

Dupré J. (2008) 'What genes are and why there are no genes for race', in Koenig B., Lee S.-J. and Richardson S. (eds) *Revisiting Race in a Genomic Age*, New Brunswick, NJ: Rutgers University Press

Dutt R. (1991) *Towards a Black Perspective in Child Protection*, London: Race Equality Unit

Dutt R. and Phillips M. (2000) 'Assessing black children in need and their families', in Department of Health, *Assessing Children in Need and their Families*, London: The Stationery Office

Dutt R. and Sanyal A. (1991) ' "Openness" in adoption or open adoption? – a black perspective', *Adoption & Fostering*, 15:4, pp 111–15

Evan B. Donaldson Institute (2009) *Finding Families for African American Children*, available at www.adoptioninstitute.org

Farmer E. and Moyers S. (2008) *Kinship Care: Fostering effective family and friends placements*, London: Jessica Kingsley Publishers

Flynn R. (2000) 'Black carers for white children', *Adoption & Fostering*, 24:1, pp 47–52

Frazer L. and Selwyn J. (2005) 'Why are we waiting? The demography of adoption for children of black, Asian and black mixed parentage in England', *Child & Family Social Work*, 10:2, pp 135–147

Gilroy P. (1990) 'The end of anti-racism', in Ball W. and Solomos J. (eds) *Race and Local Politics*, Basingstoke: Macmillan

Gray B. (2002) 'Emotional labour and befriending in family support and child protection in Tower Hamlets', *Child & Family Social Work*, 7, pp 13–22

Hall S. (1992) 'New ethnicities', in Donald J. and Rattansi A. (eds) *'Race', Culture, Difference*, London: Routledge

Harman V. and Barn R. (2005) 'Exploring the discourse concerning white mothers of mixed parentage children', in Okitikpi T. (ed) *Working with Children of Mixed Parentage*, Lyme Regis: Russell House Publishing, pp 102–111

Haslanger S. (2008) 'A social constructionist analysis of Race', in Koenig B., Lee S.-J. and Richardson S. (eds) *Revisiting Race in a Genomic Age*, New Brunswick, NJ: Rutgers University Press, pp 56–69

Hayes P. (2003) 'Giving due consideration to ethnicity in adoption placements: a principled approach,' *Child and Family Law Quarterly*, 15:3, pp 255–268

Humphreys C., Atkar S. and Baldwin N. (1999) 'Discrimination in child protection work: recurring themes in work with Asian families', *Child & Family Social Work*, 4, pp 283–291

Hunt J., Macleod A. and Thomas C. (1999) *The Last Resort: Child protection, the courts and the Children Act*, London: The Stationery Office

Ifekwunigwe J. (ed) (2004) *Mixed Race Studies*, London: Routledge

Ivaldi G. (1998) *Children Adopted from Care*, London: BAAF

Ivaldi G. (2000) *Surveying Adoption*, London: BAAF

Katz I. (1996) *The Construction of Racial Identity in Mixed Parentage Children: Mixed metaphors*, London: Jessica Kingsley Publishers

Korbin J. (2002) 'Culture and child maltreatment: cultural competence and beyond', *Child Abuse and Neglect*, 26, pp 637–644

Lewontin R. (1972) 'The apportionment of human diversity', *Evolutionary Biology*, 6, pp 381–398

Lowe N., Murch M., Borkowski M., Bader K., Copner R., Lisles C. and Shearman J. (2002) *The Plan for the Child: Adoption or long-term fostering*, London: BAAF

Macey M. (1995) 'Same race adoption policy: anti-racism or racism?', *Journal of Social Policy*, 24:4, pp 473–491

Marks J. (2008) 'Race: past, present and future', in Koenig B., Lee S.-J. and Richardson S. (eds) *Revisiting Race in a Genomic Age*, New Brunswick, NJ: Rutgers University Press, pp 21–38

Masson J., Pearce J. and Bader K. (2008) *Care Profiling Study*, London: Ministry of Justice, Research Series 4/08

Maximé J. (1993) 'The importance of racial identity for the psychological well-being of black children', *ACPP Review and Newsletter*, 15:4, pp 173–179

McRoy R. (2009) 'Children from care CAN be adopted', in Wrobel G. and Neil E. (eds) *International Advances in Adoption Research for Practice*, Chichester: Wiley-Blackwell, pp 97–118

Modood T. (1994) 'Political blackness and British Asians', *Journal of the British Sociological Association*, 4 (November), pp 859–876

Modood T., Berthoud R., Lakey J., Nazroo J., Smith P., Virdee S. and Beishon S. (1997) *The Fourth National Survey of Ethnic Minorities: Ethnic minorities in Britain – diversity and disadvantage*, London: Policy Studies Institute

Neil E. (2000) 'The reasons why young children are placed for adoption: findings from a recently placed sample and a discussion of implications for subsequent identity development', *Child and Family Social Work*, 5:4, pp 303–316

NSPCC (2007) *'Family Honour' Dilemma for British Asians Reporting Child Abuse*, available at: www.nspcc.org.uk/whatwedo/mediacentre/pressreleases/ 2007_19_march_family_honour_dilemma_for_british_asians_reporting_child_a buse_wdn43191.html

REFERENCES

Olumide J. (2002) *Raiding the Gene Pool: The social construction of mixed race*, London: Pluto Press

O'Neale V. (2000) *Excellence not Excuses: Inspections of services for ethnic minority children and families*, London: Department of Health

Oriti B., Bibb A. and Mahboubi J. (1996) 'Family centred practice with racially/ethnically mixed families', *Families in Society*, 77:9, pp 573–582

Owen C. and Statham J. (2009) *Disproportionality in Child Welfare*, London: Thomas Coram Research Unit, Department for Children, Schools and Families. Available at www.dcsf.gov.uk/research/data/uploadfiles/DCSF-RR124.pdf

Owusu-Bempah K. (2005) 'Mulatto, marginal man, half-caste, mixed race: the one drop rule in professional practice', in Okitikpi T. (ed) *Working with Children of Mixed Parentage*, Lyme Regis: Russell House Publishing, pp. 27–44

Parker D. and Song M. (eds) (2001) *Rethinking Mixed Race*, London: Pluto Press

Performance and Innovation Unit (2000) *Prime Minister's Review of Adoption*, London: Department of Health

Phillips T. (2007) Speech available at www.number10.gov.uk/Page10555.asp

Platt L. (2009) *Ethnicity and Family: Relationships within and between ethnic groups*, Harlow: University of Essex, Report to the Equality and Human Rights Commission

Prevatt-Goldstein B. (1999) 'Black, with a white parent: a positive and achievable identity', *British Journal of Social Work*, 29, pp 285–301

Prevatt-Goldstein B. (2000) 'Refocusing the "same race" debate', *Adoption & Fostering*, 24:1, pp 3–4

Quinton D. *et al* (forthcoming) *Matching in Adoptions from Care: A conceptual and research review*, London: BAAF

Richards A. and Ince I. (2000) *Overcoming Obstacles: Looked after children – quality services for black and minority ethnic children and their families*, London: Family Rights Group

Rockquemore K. A. and Laszloffy T. (2005) *Raising Biracial Children*, Lanham: Alta Mira Press

Rushton A. and Minnis H. (1997) 'Annotation: transracial family placements', *Journal of Child Psychology & Psychiatry*, 38:2, pp 147–59

Rutter M. (1989) *Scientific Foundations of Developmental Psychiatry*, London: Heinemann

233

Scorer R. (2005) 'Child abuse cases in the Muslim community', *Childright*, 221, pp 6–7

Scourfield J., Evans J., Shah W. and Beynon H. (2002) 'Responding to the experiences of minority ethnic children in virtually all-white communities', *Child and Family Social Work*, 7, pp 161–175

Selwyn J., Sturgess W., Quinton D., and Baxter C. (2006) *Costs and Outcomes of Non-infant Adoptions*, London: BAAF

Sewell T., Epstein D., Elwood J., Hey V. and Maw J. (eds) (1998) 'Loose canons: exploding the myth of the "black macho" lad', *Failing boys? Issues in gender and achievement*, Berkshire: Open University Press

Sinclair I., Baker C., Lee J. and Gibbs I. (2007) *The Pursuit of Permanency*, London: Jessica Kingsley Publishers

Small J. (2000) 'Ethnicity and placement', *Adoption & Fostering*, 24:1, pp 9–13

Sunmonu Y. (2000) 'Why black carers are deterred from adoption', *Adoption & Fostering*, 24:1, pp 59–60

Thanki V. (1994) 'Ethnic diversity and child protection', *Children and Society*, 3, pp 85–93

Thoburn J., Chand A. and Proctor J. (2005) *Child Welfare Services for Minority Ethnic Families*, London: Jessica Kingsley Publishers

Thoburn J., Norford L. and Rashid S. P. (2000) *Permanent Family Placement for Children of Minority Ethnic Origin*, London: Jessica Kingsley Publishers

Thomas A. and Chess S. (1977) *Temperament and Development*, New York, NY: Brunnel/Mazel

Tikly L., Caballero C., Haynes J. and Hill J. (2004) *Understanding the Educational Needs of Mixed Heritage Pupils*, London: DCSF, Research Report RR549

Tizard B. and Phoenix A. (2002) *Black, White or Mixed Race? Race and racism in the lives of young people of mixed parentage*, London: Routledge

Twine F. W. (1999) 'Bearing blackness in Britain: the meaning of racial difference for white birth mothers of African-descent children', *Social Identities*, 5:2, pp 185–210

Twine F. W. (2004) 'A white side of black Britain: the concept of racial literacy', *Ethnic and Racial Studies*, 27:6, pp 878–907

Vonk M. (2001) 'Cultural competence for transracial adoptive parents', *Social Work*, 16:3, pp 246–254

Ward H., Munro E., Dearden C. and Nicholoson D. (2003) *Outcomes for Looked After Children: Life pathways and decision-making for young children in care or accommodation*, Loughborough: CFR

Wehrly B. (2003) 'Breaking barriers for multiracial individuals and families', in Harper F. and McFadden J. (eds) *Culture and Counseling: New approaches*, Heights, MA: Allyn & Bacon

Williams C. and Soydan H. (2005) 'When and how does ethnicity matter?', *British Journal of Social Work*, 35:6, pp 901–920

Wilson J. (1987) *Mixed Race Children: A study of identity*, London: Allen and Unwin

Wood M. (2009) 'Mixed ethnicity, identity and adoption: research, policy and practice', *Child & Family Social Work*, advance access published online: June 10 2009

Woods R. (2008) 'When rewards and consequences fail: a case study of a primary school rule breaker', *International Journal of Qualitative Studies in Education*, 21:2, pp 181–196

Youdell D. (2003) 'Identity traps, or how black students fail', *British Journal of Sociology of Education*, 24:1, pp 3–20

Appendix I

Terms and definitions

The terms used in this study are controversial and have been the focus of heated political and academic debate. The research team have drawn on Bhopal's (2004) specific definitions of different ethnic groups and used definitions taken from the online *Blackwell Encyclopaedia of Sociology*, available at: www.sociologyencyclopedia.com/public/

Culture

The idea of culture has long been both capacious and ambiguous, due to its complex historical origins and intellectual development, and cultural analysis was not generally considered central to sociological inquiry for much of the 20th century. However, sociologists now think of culture as human processes of meaning-making, generating artefacts, categories, norms, values, practices, rituals, symbols, world views, ideas, ideologies, and discourses. They currently identify and analyse three different types of influence on meaning-making: institutional production, interactional process, and textual structure, emphasising each dimension to different degrees according to empirical topic and theoretical perspective, and often debating their relative importance.

It is increasingly recognised that culture is not static and fixed. Within any group there will be individuals who do not go along with the norms and values of that culture – individuals who challenge and behave differently. The process of learning is emphasised in considering culture and therefore the way in which culture is taught and reproduced are important components. Culture also shifts over time to accommodate new ways of thinking and being, so some of what is taught is lost and therefore culture exists in a constant state of change. Culture can be an important aspect of people's lives but it is fluid, variable and dynamic (Korbin, 2002). Culture both embraces and resists change.

Cultural competence

This term is now widely used and refers to the need for social care professionals to develop abilities to cross cultural boundaries. There is debate about how best to achieve this and whether on its own it will reduce discrimination. The term includes practice that is geared towards obtaining the knowledge and skills to work with different groups; it has a political component in promoting empowerment and inclusion. Some writers (e.g. Twine, 2004) use the term "racial literacy" to describe the process whereby white parents develop the skills to manage their mixed ethnicity child's identity.

Ethnicity

The ancient Greek word *ethnos*, the root of "ethnicity," referred to people living and acting together in a manner that we might apply to a "people" or a "nation": a collectivity with a "way of life" – some manners and mores, practices and purposes – in common, whose members share something in terms of "culture". Ethnicity always involves ethnic relations: connections and contacts between people who are seen to be different, as well as between those who are seen to be the same. A sense of ethnicity can only arise in the context of relationships and interaction with others: without difference, there is no similarity. Defining "us" implies – if nothing stronger – an image of "them". Instead of searching for ever more precise definitions, a better approach might suggest that communal, local, regional, national, and "racial" identities are locally and historically specific variations on a generic principle of collective identification: ethnicity. Each says something about "the social organisation of culture difference" and "the cultural organisation of social difference". They are culturally imagined and socially consequential, a way of phrasing the matter which recognises that distinctions between "the cultural" and "the social" may not be particularly helpful. These communal, local, regional, national, and "racial" identities also offer the possibility of "collectively ratified personal identity". They may make a considerable personal difference to individuals, both in their sense of self and in their judgement and treatment of others.

This broad understanding of ethnicity acknowledges that ethnic identification is a contextually variable and relative process. That ethnicity may be negotiable, flexible, and variable in its significance from one situation to another is among the most important lessons of the specialist social science literature (Cornell, 1996). This also means that, depending on cultural context and social situation, ethnicity may not be negotiable. There may not be much of a choice. And when ethnicity matters to people, it has the capacity to really matter, to move them to action and awaken powerful emotions.

Ethnic group

Ethnic groups are fundamental units of social organisation, which consist of members who define themselves, or are defined, by a sense of common historical origins that may also include religious beliefs, a similar language, or a shared culture. Their continuity over time as distinct groups is achieved through the intergenerational transmission of culture, traditions, and institutions.

"Race"

There is a consensus among scholars that "race" is a socially defined category that has no biological significance, despite lingering popular beliefs that still regard "races" as biological groups made up of a people with a distinct genetic heritage. There is no scientific evidence to support these notions. The importance of social factors in the creation of and perpetuation of racial categories has led to a broadening of the concept and has made "race" and ethnicity increasingly similar.

Census 2001 classifications

Different classifications, both formal and informal, are used in the UK. Perhaps the most accepted is the National Statistics classification (identical to that used in the 2001 Census in England and Wales) which contains the following groups and which were used in this study.

- White: British
- White: Irish
- White: Other
- Mixed: White and Black Caribbean
- Mixed: White and Black African
- Mixed: White and Asian
- Mixed: Other
- Asian: Pakistani
- Asian: Indian
- Asian: Sri Lankan
- Asian: Bangladeshi
- Asian: Maldivian Asian: Nepalese
- Black or Black British: Black Caribbean
- Black or Black British: Black African
- Black or Black British: Other
- Chinese or Other: Chinese
- Chinese or Other: Other

Different classifications were used in the 1991 Census in England and Wales, and in the 2001 Census in Scotland and Northern Ireland.

Although the classification is the most commonly used, it is not without controversy. At the time of the 2001 Census, when the existence and nature of such a classification became more widely known, there was much debate about whether this information was helpful and useful in the provision of services (Bhopal, 2004). For the first time, in the 2001 Census, the category "mixed" was added and allowed people to define themselves and/or their children in this way. It is not entirely clear whether someone with a white skin born in India would define themselves as Indian or "white other". The term "white Irish" has also replaced "born in Ireland", so it is no longer clear whether the new category means born or residing in Ireland or whether it is language or self-attribution that determines category. This makes it difficult for a person of minority ethnicity who thinks of themselves as "Irish" to define themselves in that way. The large population of Kurds, Cypriots, Persians and Turks are also hidden in probably the "Chinese or other" category. The Muslim Council of Britain (among many others) has campaigned for greater refinement of ethnic categories as an aid in campaigning for the removal of inequalities, exclusion, discrimination, in planning the location of community facilities, and in promoting socio-political engagement.

Appendix II

Table A1

Ethnicities of the minority ethnic children and their adopters (n = 71)

	Ethnicity of the child	*n (Ethnicities of 1st and 2nd adopters)*
Black	Black African (n = 2)	2 (Black African, Black African)
	Black Caribbean (n = 3)	1 (White British, Black African)
		2 (Black Caribbean)
Asian	Pakistani (n = 7)	6 (Pakistani, Pakistani)
		1 (Pakistani, Black Cribbean)
	Bangladeshi (n = 1)	1 (Indian, Indian)
	Asian Other (n = 1)	1 (Indian, Indian)
Mixed	White and Black	1 (White and Black Caribbean, White and
	Caribbean (n = 22)	black Caribbean)
		2 (White British, Black Caribbean)
		1 (White Other, Black Caribbean)
		1 (White British, White and Black Caribbean)
		6 (White British, White British)
		1 (White Other, White Irish)
		2 (Black Caribbean, White British)
		2 (Black Caribbean, Black Caribbean)
		1 (Black Caribbean, White and Black
		Caribbean)
		1 (Black Caribbean)
		3 (White British)
		1 (Black African)
	White and Black	1 (Black African, White British)
	African (n = 2)	1 (White and Black Caribbean)
	White And Asian	4 (White British, White and Asian)
	(n = 17)	4 (White British, White British)
		2 (White British, Indian)
		3 (Pakistani, Pakistani)
		1 (Pakistani, Not recorded)
		1 (White Irish, Indian)
		1 (White Other, White British)
		1 (White British)

Ethnicity of the child	*n (Ethnicities of 1st and 2nd adopters)*
Mixed Other (n = 16)	5 (White British, White British)
	1 (White British, White British)
	1 (White British, White Other)
	1 (White British, White and Asian)
	1 (White British, Other)
	1 (Black African, White Other)
	1 (Pakistani, White British)
	1 (Mixed Other, White British)
	1 (Mixed Other, White Other)
	1 (White British)
	1 (Black African)
	1 (Pakistani)

Table A2

Faiths of the minority ethnic children and their adopters (n = 71)

Child's faith	*n (Faiths of 1st and 2nd adopters)*
Christian (n = 7)	3 (Christian, Christian) 1 (Muslim, Christian) 1 (Christian) 1 (No religion) 1 (Not recorded)
Muslim (n = 16)	12 (Muslim, Muslim) 1 (Christian, Christian) 1 (Not recorded, Not recorded) 1 (Christian) 1 (Muslim)
No particular faith (n = 36)	20 (Christian, Christian) 2 (Jewish, Muslim) 2 (Not recorded, Not recorded) 2 (No religion, No religion) 1 (No religion, Not recorded) 1 (Orthodox Christian, Christian) 1 (Other Christian, Other Christian) 1 (Muslim, Muslim) 1 (Muslim, Not recorded) 4 (Christian) 1 (No religion)
Not recorded (n = 12)	6 (Christian, Christian) 1 (Muslim, Christian) 1 (Hindu, Christian) 1 (Not recorded, No religion) 1 (Not recorded, Not recorded) 2 (Christian)

Table A3

Languages of the minority ethnic children and their adopters (n = 71)

Child's language	n (Languages of 1st and 2nd adopters)
Multilingual (including English as the first language) (n = 5)	4 (Multilingual, Multilingual) 1 (English, English)
English (n = 60)	40 (English English) 1 (English, Not recorded) 3 (Multilingual, English) 1 (Multilingual, Not recorded) 2 (Multilingual, Multilingual) 1 (Not recorded, Not recorded) 8 (English) 2 (Multilingual) 1 (Not recorded)
Bengali/Sylheti (n = 1)	1 (Multilingual, Multilingual)
Punjabi (n = 1)	1 (Multilingual, Multilingual)
Pashto (Afghanistan) (n = 1)	1 (Pashto, Pashto)
Not recorded (n = 3)	2 (Multilingual, Multilingual) 1 (English)

Table A4
The coefficients for the final multivariate binary logistic regression model

Covariate	Coefficient (b_i)	OR $[exp(b_i)]$	95% CI	P-*value*
Age at panel				
0–1 year				
(reference category)				
1–3 years	−.497	.608	(.216–1.714)	.347
>3 years	−1.959	.141	(.053–.374)	.000
Child's ethnicity				
Mixed				
(reference category)				
Black	−.903	.406	(.104–1.583)	.194
Asian	−1.356	.258	(.093–.714)	.009

p values refer to comparisons with reference group; OR = Odds ratio;
CI = Confidence Interval

Table A5
The coefficients for the final multivariate binary logistic regression model

Covariate	Coefficient (b_i)	ARR $[exp(b_i)]$	95% CI	P-*value*
Age at panel				
0–1 year				
(reference category)				
1–3 years	−.342	.710	(.409–1.233)	.224
>3 years	−1.365	.255	(.130–.501)	.000

p values refer to comparisons with reference group; ARR = Adoption Rate
Ratio; CI = Confidence Interval

Table A6
The coefficients for the final multivariate binary logistic regression model

Covariate	Coefficient (b_i)	ARR $[exp(b_i)]$	95% CI	P-*value*
Age at panel				
0–1 year (reference category)				
1–3 years	−.693	.500	(.331–.803)	.004
>3 years	−1.376	.253	(.144–.443)	.000
Child's ethnicity				
White (reference category)				
Black	−1.026	.358	(.125–1.028)	.056
Asian	−.870	.419	(.197–.890)	.024
Mixed	−.276	.758	(.479–1.201)	.238

p values refer to comparisons with reference group; ARR = Adoption Rate Ratio; CI = Confidence Interval

Figure A1
Number of weeks from the time of the adoption recommendation to placement or change of plan

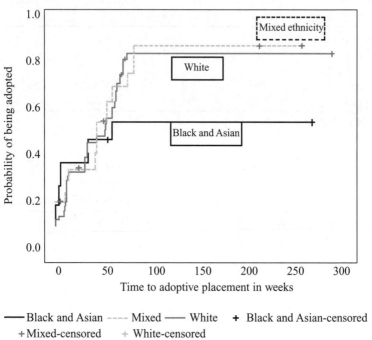

Black and Asian —–– Mixed —— White   **+** Black and Asian-censored
+ Mixed-censored   + White-censored

Figure A2
Predicted time to adoption for children by the age at the time of the adoption recommendation

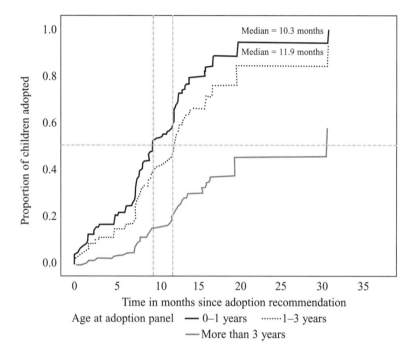

Figure A3
Predicted time to adoption according to age

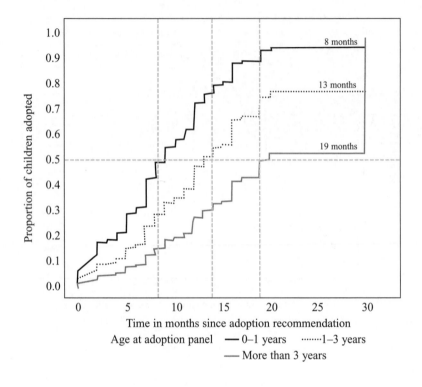

Figure A4
Predicted time to adoption according to ethnicity

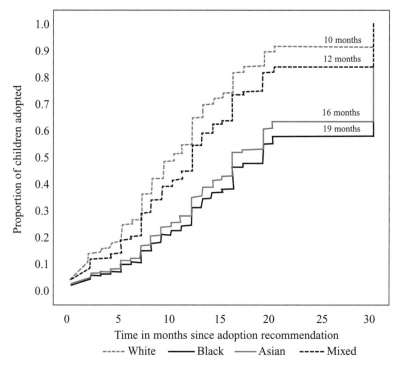

Index

Compiled by Elisabeth Pickard